Readings

Readings

GAYATRI CHAKRAVORTY SPIVAK

LONDON NEW YORK CALCUTTA

Seagull Books, 2014

© Gayatri Chakravorty Spivak, 2014

Foreword © Lara Choksey, 2014

ISBN 978 0 8574 2 208 8

British Library Cataloguing-in-Publication Data
A catalogue record for this book is available from the British Library.

Typeset in Scala and ScalaSans by Seagull Books, Calcutta, India
Printed and bound by Maple Press, York, Pennsylvania, USA

CONTENTS

ACKNOWLEDGEMENT

I could not have done this book without Lara Choksey.

Gayatri Chakravorty Spivak

EDITOR'S NOTE

The substance of this book is taken from a series of seminars given at the University of Pune from 23 to 26 May 2012, at the invitation of Professor Aniket Jaaware. Our thanks to him for his help with this project.

FOREWORD

This book stands in for a series of responses between student and teacher. In May 2012, Gayatri Chakravorty Spivak spent four days conducting seminars with students at the University of Pune, making herself responsible to them in a scene of teaching. The seminars sit between talk and class, the students unknown but the lessons rigorous and personal, performed by a migrant teacher in the country of her passport: 'At Pune, I found myself speaking citizen to citizen,'[1] she relates. From here came readings of Frantz Fanon's *Black Skin, White Masks*, J. M. Coetzee's *Summertime*, Elizabeth Gaskell's *North and South* and rereadings of her own essays, 'Righting Wrongs' and 'Three Women's Texts and a Critique of Imperialism'.

The lecture hall at Pune became a text, read by Spivak as she responded to the students. *Readings* may seem to give lessons only within the borders of India, addressed to future

---

1 Gayatri Chakravorty Spivak, 'The Practice of Freedom Is Not Impractical' (plenary lecture for the Annual Conference, L'Association Internationale de Littérature Comparée [AILC/ICLA], University of Paris-Sorbonne, France, 20 July 2013).

trainers of 'Indian' imaginations, a skills exchange between citizens, but Spivak is also following a different set of rules. She marks out her identification with the situation—'constituting a subject in error'—while suggesting the possibility of moving beyond it. She assigns herself a place within borders to demonstrate how she might reach the no-place of a borderless world: a task that requires mediating destruction.

While editing this book, I reported for the *Statesman* on the eviction of several hundred people from a site in east Calcutta. The Kolkata Municipal Development Authority (KMDA) tried to clear unauthorized inhabitants from the site, so that a developer could build a complex on it. Most of the people evicted were daily-wage labourers and their families who had settled on the site in temporary shelters. Rather than leave the site on notice of their eviction, the people campaigned for shelter. They held demonstrations and a hunger strike, and issued requests for rehabilitation to the state government. The state responded with violence: beatings, surveillance and imprisonment. The people remained.

The then-chairman of the KMDA justified the state's refusal to offer alternative shelter by invoking the Constitution of India. 'There is nothing in the Constitution that says these people have a right to shelter,' he said, standing outside the 10-foot-high concrete wall that the KMDA had constructed around the site and its inhabitants. 'Haven't you read it properly?' he asked me.

The chairman referred to Article 19 of the Constitution's Right to Freedom section. Two of the article's subclauses describe the right of citizens to 'move freely throughout' and to 'reside and settle in any part of' the territory of India. Citizens are free to exercise these rights, while also subject to 'reasonable restrictions' that can be enacted 'either in the interests of the general public or for the protection of Scheduled Tribes.'[2]

If I had read the Constitution in the proper way, I would have understood that the chairman was imposing 'reasonable restrictions' on those claiming a right to settle 'in the interests of the general public,' carrying out the function of his assigned place as municipal administrator. In the municipal reading, this 'general public' did not include the people evicted. It was not the chairman's place to contest this reading but to translate it into practice. The people evicted were caught in a place outside constitutional provision, without alternative and with no right to remain.

The story becomes fixed as commonplace, an available example of the bordering of territory. What good can a local rereading do, if the municipal interpretation is already translated as exclusionary policy?

At Pune, the students described comparable situations, expressing a sense of general hopelessness at a national model of development. 'What can be done?' they asked.

Rather than offer a general solution, Spivak suggests a form of risk-taking, intimate and without guarantees, a

2 Article 19, *Constitution of India* (1950). Available at: http://lawmin.nic.in/-olwing/coi/coi-english/Const.Pock%202Pg.Rom8Fsss(6).pdf (last accessed 16 April 2014).

negotiation between thought and act out of which a possible practice of freedom might emerge. Such intimate risk-taking takes place in a mode that might enable the will to be realized well, where the universalizable might be derived by chance through careful attention to the particular, one at work towards the other.

In a deferred response to the chairman's question, I attempt a careful, though improper reading of the Constitution's Right to Freedom section, imagining its appropriation by the people evicted. By remaining on the site in east Calcutta, they offered a lesson on inhabiting a restricted zone, 'living without authorization,' using 'borrowed resources.'[3] I imagine them reading the Right to Freedom section if not properly, then cautiously, acknowledging their displacement from it. Then I see the group 'prepared to be carried off by its own intimate risk-taking'[4] with the code of the Constitution, individuals inserting themselves as a temporary collective into the bracket of (general public), without authorization. Re-entering through this counter-reading, I perceive an act of equivalence. Through this, the evicted people move from their assigned place in the municipal reading of the Constitution, where they live outside legitimacy, to a place not allocated to them, suggesting their inclusion within legal settlement. The code of the Constitution is transformed into

3 Gayatri Chakravorty Spivak, 'Reading *De la grammatologie*', preface to *Reading Derrida's 'Of Grammatology'* (Sean Gaston and Ian Maclachlan eds) (London: Bloomsbury Academic, 2011), pp. *xxix–xxxix*; here, p. *xxxii*.

4 Ibid.

a crossing place, and a local gap in national provision is exposed. This intimate risk-taking operates in a different field from nation-building on reclaimed national territory. It neither constructs its own laws, nor tries to destroy those already in existence, but becomes complicit with the restriction of space in language in order to move around it.

Is this Spivak's task at Pune? She constructs herself as metropolitan migrant, a subject position suggested to her by the text of the lecture hall. She offers this stereotype as, in her words, 'a needed political protection against possibilizing a past as preferred or desired influence.' In character, she lays out a struggle of nationalist identitarianism in India: on one hand, denying English for the sake of seamless nation-building and with it, access to a certain kind of borderlessness; on the other, ignoring Indian languages in favour of nationalized global membership, for which English is a prerequisite. She encourages the students to use their training in English studies to enter other Indian languages, that by doing so they might encounter 'the principle of invented equivalence,' and undermine the 'possessiveness, the exclusiveness, the isolationist expansionism of mere nationalism.'[5]

Describing the history that leads her to this construction of herself, acting out this stereotype in the text at Pune, she moves beyond it to suggest a task of 'worlding': making a world, turning insight into instrument, through and into a

---

5 Gayatri Chakravorty Spivak, 'Nationalism and the Imagination' in *An Aesthetic Education in the Era of Globalization* (Cambridge, MA: Harvard University Press, 2012), pp. 275–300; here, p. 285.

possible practice of freedom. In this task, language borders can trace the hidden frontiers of common places. The lessons here disclose a restricted language, inviting a reader to negotiate movement—fraught with error—between text and field.

Lara Choksey
April 2014

INTRODUCTION

'Spivak doesn't talk about India enough.' And in New York: 'Well, you know, she doesn't seem to belong to New York.' As a Bengali, I often move, however unwillingly, under the influence of Tagore. This is the one hundred and fiftieth birth anniversary of Tagore, and this middle-class Bengali says: *Deshe deshe mor ghor achhe*—I have a place from country to country, a place, a room. *Ghor* in Bengali and *ghar* in Hindi are not quite the same. A language border, and as we travel south, the borders are less permeable. For a very long time, I have worried that there is no serious comparative literature across the North–South divide in India. There is no market for it.

We are a borderless country in English. For some of us, it is a borderless country. My earliest childhood as an Indian and a Bengali was scarred by bordering, of another kind. I was born in British India. Partition in 1947. I saw that border, as I walked across Toba Tek Singh between Bangladesh and India.[1] On uneven ground, in yellow paint on a block of wood, in Bengali script, was painted *Bharat*. I looked back and there

1 Saadat Hasan Manto, 'Toba Tek Singh' (Khalid Hasan trans.) in *Memories of Madness: Stories of 1947* (New Delhi: Penguin India, 2002), pp. 517–23.

was a sun-bleached blue wooden signboard proclaiming *Gono-prajatantrik Bangladesh Sarkar*. And in-between was Toba Tek Singh. I crossed the border of Bangladesh to the Indian border post, and half-educated Indian officials demanded a visa from me into my own country. I carry an Indian passport. Here was a class border. Only the Bangladeshi underclass crossed the Darshana–Gede border to board the all third-class train into Sealdah Station, Calcutta.

This is a relatively benign example of class borders. I mention class apartheid that I witness in my own state of West Bengal, in my writing. Class apartheid is not just in my rural schools. It is between the rural underclass as a whole and everything above. This class apartheid in education that I have witnessed in my state now for nearly 30 years is not, I hope, replicated in all the states of India, but I fear it may be. It is a displacement of the millennial caste borders that is one of the disgraces of India. All of this is of course complicated by the gender borders we share with the rest of humanity. But the caste border crosses race, class and gender. We live, then, with many internal borders in India, as elsewhere in the world. Such borders are specific to every civilization, every history. They work in our everyday, as they work in the macrologies across the narratives of history, and I look at one of them below when I read a couple of poems.

What is a border? It is, of course, the geographic limits outlining the nation-states, often conflictually. We add to those the internal borders of class and gender, of caste, and the right to health, education, welfare and intellectual, rather

than only manual, labour. When I was undergoing the tribu-
lations of Partition, I was not old enough to think Africa. Now
I know that the arbitrarily drawn borders that violated African
principles of space and made borderlessness impossible
would take the Indian discussion into different directions.
For we as children, confined to thinking our corner of the
world as the World, experienced friendship across borders
when Nehru and Zhou Enlai held hands, until the McMahon
Line—the border set by the British—created conflict.

In 1961, I left India. The India–China conflict occurred
in 1962. Hearing about the war in India, I thought borders
were fictions. I thought, for the first time, that the earth came
unmarked, except by natural boundaries. I look at Palestine,
at Kashmir festering, and mark how history complicates this
bit of common sense. And therefore, all facts to the contrary
—we who learn from fiction must think a borderless world
of unconditional hospitality.

Why do we have to do this? I used to think that this is
because human beings are born ethical. Or at least they
develop an ethical sign system as they learn their first language as infants, before reason. I am still somewhat sure of
this, but I think the possible impulse towards the ethical has
to be activated away from the underived selfishness which
also operates in all creaturely life. I say 'creaturely life'
because I try not to be a human racist. In this activation, a literary education can be a great help, because the teacher
engages directly with the imagination. The teacher of literature has nothing else to teach. If we teach literary history, it

is on the model of history as a discipline. If we teach literature as evidence—and even Frantz Fanon uses it as evidence—it is on the legal model and so on. But by ourselves, we have nothing else to engage with than training the imagination.

It is only with the help of the training of the imagination that we can change our epistemological performance. In other words, we change how we construct objects for knowing. And engaging with the imagination in the simplest way makes us suspend our own interests into the language that is happening in the text, the text of another traced voice, the voice of the presumed producer of the text. I use these words 'trace', 'text', 'voice' because the utility of the imagination is not confined to what we recognize as 'literature' today. The element that we might call the 'literary', that trains the imagination to step out of self-interest, exists in many shapes and forms in the pasts of all civilizations. In the thinking of a borderless world today, we have to use the imagination through literary training in the broadest sense, including the filmic, the videographic, the hypertextual, learning to read in the broadest sense.

It is the task of the imagination to place a question mark upon the declarative. Imaginative training for epistemological performance focuses upon the detail that often escapes the attention of people who work to solve what seem to be more immediate problems. I draw your attention to the poet and the lawyer in the exchange of letters between Tagore and Gandhi. Tagore is resolute, saying that the only way in which imaginations can come together is through *bajey kharoch*— wasteful spending—spending not on one's own behalf;

whereas Gandhi says: 'My experience has proved to my satisfaction that literary training by itself adds not an inch to one's moral height and that character-building is independent of literary training.'[2]

This exchange is important: it is the task of the imagination to place a question mark on the declarative. Imaginative training for epistemological performance focuses on the detail that often escapes the attention of people who work to solve what seem to be more immediate problems. And no revolution lasts or prospers if there is no attention to detail. This is particularly important, because everything that is medicine can turn to poison if the person or the collectivity who is using it is not trained to know how much to use, when and how. This is the training of the imagination that makes revolutions last. It refers not to broad political descriptives but to the micrology of practice.

This comes clear with so-called corporate social responsibility. There may be certain showcased features within a private enterprise where social responsibility is evident, but private enterprise today is held within the performative contradiction of borderless capital, and thus it is not possible for it to use its financial and economic policy maximally for the welfare of the state and its people and for the welfare of the world. Social responsibility, therefore, is often a calculation of how much capitalism can get away with.

2 Mohandas K. Gandhi, 'The Poet's Anxiety' in Sabyasachi Bhattacharya (ed.), *The Mahatma and the Poet: Letters and Debates between Gandhi and Tagore, 1915–1941* (New Delhi: National Book Trust, 1997), p. 66.

I am just coming from Croatia. A few years after the disappearance of socialism, the Balkan Forum is trying to instruct the world in the inequities of privatization. Although labour is no longer the prime mover of resistance in the globalized world, it seems to me important that the majority of the working class in a postsocialist space, as in the Balkans, is attempting such instruction. I add this to bring news from outside the India–US circuit that we otherwise would travel in. The Balkan Forum was constantly regretting that no one listens to the Balkans as a European voice. I remarked there that my closest association with the work against privatization in a labour movement was in Bangladesh. 'Do you think anybody,' I asked the Balkan Forum, 'listens to Bangladesh as a global advisor?' Suggesting, then, that they not look above, at Europe, but find collectivity among the subalterns, below.

There are many intellectuals who condone violence, and even endorse it, without much thought. Those who work for peace know that if violence is used to bring about a change in the polity and to secure borders, it will become a poisonous habit that will destroy a new nation. Once again, the training of the imagination into a will for peaceful social justice, rather than winning all conflicts by violence, may only be brought about by sustained attention to detail, and the sustained training into suspending oneself in the interest of the other person or persons.

That is what training in literary reading offers beyond the conventional definition of literature—a painstaking learning of the language of the other. This training can also come through cultural rearing, often compromised by gender and class. In other words, only women and servants must think of others, the babus and their children think of themselves, and the queer generally remain in hiding. This is a general description as I move through India. It is amazing to see in my own class how different the treatment of women and servants is, to observe how the children and the babus behave.

Literary reading can, if given the chance, undo this, and not just in India. I go to conferences all over the world and no one ever looks at who cleans the rooms. I was in Italy before I went to Croatia. I was lecturing at an old Italian socialist outfit. After the lecture, I was invited to go to La Scala and share the box of the Pradas. It was a galling evening, although the music was splendid. I returned to my hostess' house, and the only other South Asians there were the two servants, both from Sri Lanka. A literary education can direct one to noticing these otherwise ignored details. That is the question mark in the question of a borderless world. Does education in the broadest sense nurture nationalism—I don't talk enough about India, I'm not enough in New York—or a regionalism that curbs the performative contradiction of a borderless capital?

Whatever we plan, the future will deal with it in its own way. We must make room for this undecidability as we plan. This is the future anterior. That too is marked by the question mark. Something will have happened; we cannot now know. It is in view of the elusive future anterior, then, that we must remind ourselves that, without the general nurturing of the will to justice among the people, there can be no borderless world, no end to the power play of small and large, rich and poor, debtor and creditor nations. Any thinking of welfare-world borderlessness must attend, therefore, to education—primary through post-tertiary—at the same time as it attends to the uncoupling of specifically capitalist globalization and the nation-state. This is an almost impossible task to remember, especially when there are such complex and urgent immediate tasks lined up, but it must be repeated. Without this attention, there is no chance of the will to justice to survive political victory.

We are here in the Department of English Literature. The tradition of the teaching of English literature is strong in our country for reasons that I do not need to repeat. Unfortunately, material reasons as well as a not-unconnected devotion to English have produced a lowering of interest in the production and consumption, indeed in the quality, of work in the regional languages of India. On the other hand, I think we cannot undermine our current excellence in the study of English—throw away something that we have developed over the last few centuries—because of this situation. The real solution would be to find ways of supporting a comparative literature of Indian languages rather than to jettison the exquisite literature of global English today.

When the country became independent, we, who were among the first generation of postcolonial students and intellectuals, swore that we would see English as yet another language, rather than the language of the master. Because of the global situation, this was, of course, not possible. However, all over the world, we hear of the Asian century, so that stuff that you read about American superpower wealth as little as a few years ago is not quite true today any more. Asia here is metonymically India and China. Yet, if India is indeed one of the rising powers of the Asian century, let it not make the mistake of supporting an education that is nationalist in its ideology and capitalist in its goals. We must put on the country's agenda the slow and careful building of a will to social justice, generation after generation, within the speed required by the ceaseless strategizing for maintaining a leading role and a vanguardist control of capitalist globalization, which has been the main concern of the top levels of the ruling class in our country since the 1990s.

The radical emphasis cannot be simply on explaining the political information or claiming the right to information. Information is not enough. You have to train minds that can deal with information. Information control leads to human-interest stories in the *Economic and Political Weekly*. The radical emphasis, instead, must be on attempts to change habits of mind, for which the best weapon remains a literary education, best developed worldwide in the study of English literature, not even French or German. It is in this context that I have talked about the concept of affirmative sabotage, a concept we will develop in the next chapters.

We must learn to demand more financial support for a comparative literature of the Indian languages. Elsewhere, I have called this kind of demand a concern for the ethical healthcare of a nation at war with general injustice. This would promote a kind of borderlessness while preserving linguistic borders as crossing places rather than indications of impenetrability. I do not know if I will see this in my lifetime, but I continue to repeat this, especially to students. From the place of a victim of globalization, I propose moving to being a borderless Indian of a certain kind, invoking a performative contradiction which must attend carefully to borders, the very ground of an enlightened comparative literature in which English remains a medium.

When we undertake to find this utopia—which can of course never be found—we realize that a borderless world already exists where capital roams free. The present financial crisis in the United States and Europe was occasioned by unregulated capital attempting to turn finance capital over and across borders, in and out, borrowing and lending repeatedly, to increase its volume exponentially until international capital could not keep up with the risks incurred by unrestricted selling of securitized loans. Such crossing of borders needs to keep borders intact. It seeks to preserve the difference between nation-state-based currencies, further divided by the global North, the G20 and the global South. Without this, the currency speculation, which is the base of finance capital, such as practised by renowned philanthropists like George Soros, for example, would not flourish. These virtual and electronic divisions are added to more conventional borders so that capital can travel across borders in a digitally borderless fashion. We, the organic intellectuals of globalization, can use this as a model of comparative literature, undoing the crisis by imaginative training. This, too, is a species of affirmative sabotage.

Borderlessness, in an extra-moral sense, needs borders of a certain sort in order to be borderless. It is within this performative contradiction that the entire problematic of immigration—which you cannot ignore if you live in the United States—is lodged. I remind you of the lines going round blocks at the American Embassy in New Delhi, or the lines going round blocks at the Federal Building in New York for green cards. Capital cannot let go of massively underpaid labour with no workplace safety or benefits requirement. Undocumented immigrant labour is the new subaltern social group. And yet, racialization ('They're not Euro-US') and sexualization ('They are coming into the United States to drop a baby so that they can have an American-citizen baby') must deport migrant labour. This is also a contradiction. Capital needs to keep soft currency soft. Labour must therefore cross frontiers, not borders, undercover, where hard currency beckons.

I will explain the difference between borders and frontiers, so cruel for many underclass paperless immigrants, through a joke between mother and daughter. As you know, the first European passage to the Americas happened because Columbus mistook it for the East–West passage. The general subject, the neutral subject, the Chakravortys, the name which was given to kings because they had the free wheel, the chakra that could go everywhere, that did not need a visa, as it were, has been reterritorialized into the US.

Columbus' mistake has been reversed. My mother, who was my brother's dependent, had a US passport. I don't. I would say to her, 'You Americans are the Chakravortys now. You can go everywhere.' She crossed borders travelling with me; I, frontiers. She would slip through and I would say, 'Stay close, stay close,' as they would look at my passport and my face, my passport and my face, and even sometimes ask, 'Do you have any relatives in this country?' I would say, 'Yes, right there, across the border. Let me go,' because Mother would be sitting there with her US passport. That's the difference between a frontier and a border, simply put.

I am carrying this analogy forward into the study of literature. I am suggesting that if we are obliged to become what Antonio Gramsci would call 'the organic intellectuals of capitalist globalization', let us do so in this supplementing spirit. In the best of all possible worlds, the performative contradictions of a literary borderlessness supplement the cruelties as well as the social productivity of seemingly borderless capital. We know what the outlines of supplementation are: the supplement knows the exact shape of the gap that must be filled, not any blank but a textual blank, a blank framed by a text that must be known with critical intimacy rather than from a critical distance.

Since the supplement comes from the outside, it also introduces the dangerous element of the incalculable, because the supplement is not calculated by the rules of that which it supplements. So let us think it through: global capital and literature. Literature is the element of the incalculable here. This is something we must think about. The will to social justice for all, rather than justified self-interest, introduces the element of the incalculable even in the resistance to our digitally calculable globalized world. I cannot imagine what it would be like if there were no relief map of foreign exchanges between hard and soft currencies, if capital's false promise of a level playing field were true, if utopia could be calculated. I only know that Europe's plans for creating a borderlessness within its own outlines are coming undone, as Greece is on the brink of leaving the Eurozone while Turkey enters it (although that entry seems more dubious at time of revising). If we attend to the narrative history of the millennial play of borders upon the European continent, we Brit-Lit types can plot it in terms of a literary Byzantium.

This would be a literary supplementation from a European rather than an Indian narrative, fanciful and incomprehensible to some, but I hope provocative and suggestive to others. Here is Byzantium, in the dance between Greece, Turkey and the European Union today read by a literary critic. Istanbul is the modern name of Byzantium, a corruption of Constantinople—Constantinopolis—as most people think, but its more interesting derivation is the appellation, Istinpolin, a name they heard Byzantine Greeks use, which in reality was a Greek phrase (*eiset n polin*) which meant 'in the city'.[3] Through a series of speech permutations over a span of centuries, this name became 'Istanbul', just a civic interiority, a

<hr>

3 B. E., 'Istanbul' in *Enclyclopædia Brittanica*, VOL. 22, 15th EDN (Chicago: Encyclopædia Britannica Inc., 1995), p. 148.

Medina (also a city called 'city'), Medina for ever Arabic, Istanbul for ever Greek, as is India.

Even as Greece is fracturing the Eurozone, Byzantium, the city called city, historically standing in for an empire, and then a nation-state, is sidling in. Yeats saw the mosaic that he celebrates in 'Sailing to Byzantium' in Italy, in Ravenna. Later he went to Sicily to see more examples of Byzantine work.

This gesture of finding a domesticated Byzantium, the city which had stood for the Eastern Roman Empire, now tamed as the latest entrant (perhaps) into the European Union, is an example of the phenomenon, Byzantium as place-holding proper name for the chiasmus East–West— even if it is to access eternity. It thus holds a transcendental promise, though the scene of a subduing. Yeats writes of Josef Strzygowski's *Origin of Christian Church Art* (1923):

> To him the East, as certainly to my instructors, is not India or China, but the East that has affected European civilization: Asia Minor, Mesopotamia, Egypt. From the Semitic East he derives all art which associates Christ with the attributes of royalty. It substitutes Christ Pantokrator for the bearded mild Hellenic Christ, makes the Church hierarchical and powerful.[4]

In 'Sailing to Byzantium', let us assume that Yeats is imagining a boat ride down the Mediterranean, in and round the Greek islands, reversing Odysseus' route. There is no

---

4 W. B. Yeats, 'The Great Year of the Ancients' in *A Vision* (London: Macmillan, 1962[1937]), pp. 243–66; here, p. 257.

Byzantium for Odysseus to stop at, but coming from Asia into Europe, he swings by the outpost of the Cicones tribe in Thrace, which is supposed also to be the birthplace of Orpheus, the limit of the known world for the ancient Greeks. Odysseus did not know East–West, but let me just mention in passing that for Derrida, who was Ulysses the mediterranean in one of his many polytropic self-imaginings, there was a South–North across the famous sea, redoing Augustine. A topos—about topology, moving to 'the place', like a city called city, for Augustine Rome, for Derrida, Paris, for Yeats, Byzantium. Utopias.

Yeats writes of the 'to come'. The last line of the poem —'Of what is past, or passing or to come'[5]—spells a non-accessibility to the stability of the present, a gesture, protecting from claims to influence. The present is a vanishing relationship, constituted by its vanishing. Let us look at Benjamin's powerful articulation, which I will cite again at the end. 'The past can be seized only as an image which flashes up at the instant of its recognizability, never to be seen again. [. . .] History is the object of a construction, whose site forms not with homogeneous empty time, but time filled with the now time.'[6] Yeats' time, the time for literary action, for literary activism, now time, is not a present of the sort that you can catch as something that actually exists.

5 W. B. Yeats, 'Sailing to Byzantium' in Collected Poems of W. B. Yeats (London: Collector's Library / CRW Publication, 2010), pp. 267–8.

6 Walter Benjamin, 'Theses on the Philosophy of History' in Illuminations (Harry Zohn trans.) (London: Pimlico, 1999), pp. 245–55; here, pp. 247–52, translation modified.

Many people think that 'homogeneous empty time' was a phrase coined by Benedict Anderson in *Imagined Communities* (1982), a book which does not grant us the ability to understand what we are about, or to understand the great economic and political narratives of liberation that come from Europe.[7] Many people think that Benedict Anderson wrote 'homogeneous empty time' and that Homi Bhabha opposed it, but in fact, it comes from this extraordinary passage in Benjamin where he talks about the time of action.

We know only a passing and, studying in the present, we construct a past thing. This is epistemology at work, forever trying to alter or affect, alter affect, the abreactive episteme. T. Sturge Moore noticed that although the subject of the poem claims, 'Once out of nature I shall never take / My bodily form from any natural thing,' since the poet wants to be an artificial bird, the form he chooses is from nature: 'Your *Sailing to Byzantium*,' he writes, 'as magnificent as the first three stanzas are, lets me down in the fourth, as such a goldsmith's bird is as much nature as a man's body, especially if it only sings like Homer and Shakespeare of what is past or passing or to come to Lords and Ladies.'[8]

In response, Yeats writes the turgid poem 'Byzantium', where he makes clear that the form is 'ghostly': 'I hail the

[7] Benedict Anderson, *Imagined Communities: Reflections on the Origin and Spread of Nationalism* (London: Verso, 2006[1982]). For Partha Chatterjee's critique of *Imagined Communities*, see Partha Chatterjee, *Nationalist Thought and the Colonial World: A Derivative Discourse?* (London: Zed Books for the United Nations, 1986).

[8] W. B. Yeats and T. Sturge Moore, *Their Correspondence, 1901–1937* (Ursula Bridge ed.) (London: Routledge & Kegan Paul, 1953), p. 162.

superhuman.' It is as if he is insisting: 'Look here, don't make a mistake now.' When poetry is written in this admonitory style, it is not at its best.

> I hail the superhuman;
> I call it death-in-life and life-in-death.
> Miracle, bird or golden handiwork,
> More miracle than bird or handiwork
> Planted on the star-lit golden bough,
> Can like the cocks of Hades crow,
> Or, by the moon embittered, scorn aloud
> In glory of changeless metal
> Common bird or petal
> And all complexities of mire or blood.[9]

'So don't mistake it for a "natural thing", T. Sturge Moore,' Yeats writes in effect.[10] But the mistake remained: like the mistake meant to be made by the subject of 'The Wild Swans at Coole', who thinks 59 swans, the objects of his vision, described as empirical, can fly 'lover by lover'.[11] Obviously false. Fifty-nine is an odd number. To constitute a subject in error with characteristic simplicity is another rhetorical protection against possibilizing a past as preferred or desired influence. In a more extended discussion, this can be carried through in relation to the Osmanli nostalgia/ambitions of Turkey in the Balkans today, and Greece talking about its

9 W. B. Yeats, 'Byzantium' in *Collected Poems of W. B. Yeats* (London: Collector's Library, 2010), pp. 335–6.

10 Yeats and Sturge Moore, *Their Correspondence*, p. 164.

11 W. B. Yeats, 'The Wild Swans At Coole' in *Collected Poems of W. B. Yeats* (London: Collector's Library, 2010), p. 187.

ownership of democracy as it bites the dust. Against this golden ageism in extremis, the literary constitution of a subject in error with characteristic simplicity is a needed political protection.

Speaking, then, autocritically in a spirit of alliance, I say that the idea of East–West as Byzantium, cleansed of empirical details, and attributing that cleansing to Byzantine aesthetics by projection (by the US critic Clement Greenberg, or as the Balkans and Eastern Europe in their relationship with Western Europe after the Cold War), is not adequate to what is happening in the world in the first quarter of the twenty-first century. For 'Byzantium', like all named places that have had a share in utopia, cannot be subdued. My sense of 'utopia' comes from the root meaning of the word, that it is no-place, a good place by ruse, substituting *eu* for *u* in the Greek word, to make it mean a good place—and today even a European Union place! EU, ha ha.

The city called the city has always run on the aim to achieve utopia, more or less disingenuously. It allows the ignoring of the double bind of history as the site of struggle, of the warp and woof of the tracing of history—by all but the smartest masters. As a reader of literature, I learn the lesson without mastery and, complicit with, folded into, that textile, I dream of Thrace, the home of the mythic Orpheus, uxorious to a fault, quite unlike Adam. I think of the shepherds of Thrace, which Odysseus visited, the stage for the city, which never achieved a polis. These shepherds, I muse, only half-fancifully, would then have been underived subalterns, as

Marx thought about the originary communists. For the ancient Greeks, Thrace was borderless. It was one of the four corners of Oceanus, the limit of the known.

Byzantium is not for us, then, a place of taking sides; it is a site of struggle. Septimus Severus Romanizes it, Diocletian divides it, Constantine Christianizes it, Justinian restores it, the Fourth Crusade devastates it, from 800 CE, a tug of war with the Holy Roman Empire to the west, Orthodoxy refused to join with Catholicism, East would not join West, and Byzantium became Ottoman. The tradition of tremendous regional strife, within which Yeats is symptomatic, as you read his poetry, continued, and inscribed a famous history: genocide's pogroms as empire turns to state. In 1916, Messrs Sykes and Picot, by secret understanding, wrote the 'Middle East' upon the body of Byzantium, so that the Holy Land could become a violent and violating utopia. This is also a suppression of cosmopolitanism-as-comparativism—as recorded in Wadad Makdisi Cortas' *World I Loved* (2009) and Khaled Ziadeh's *Neighbourhood and Boulevard* (2011).

Today, as Byzantium shuffles into Europe, in the process reclaiming a new avant-garde, the Osmanli East–West spirit acknowledges conflict by resolution and reclaiming. In the autumn of 2009, relations between Serbia and Bosnia, never easy since the savage civil war of the 1990s, were slipping towards outright hostility. Western mediation efforts had failed. Ahmet Davutoğlu, the foreign minister of Turkey, offered to step in. It was a complicated role for Turkey, not least because Bosnia is, like Turkey, a predominantly Muslim country and Serbia is an Orthodox Christian nation with which Turkey had long been at odds. East–West. But Davutoğlu had shaped Turkey's ambitious foreign policy according to a principle he called 'zero problems with neighbours'.[12] Neither Serbia nor Bosnia actually share a border with Turkey. Davutoğlu, however, defined his neighbourhood expansively as the vast space of former Ottoman dominion, so that this story within which Yeats occupies a place is, as I was saying, a political narrative that has economico-political sense for us today. This Osmanli impulse, with resistance from within, continues under Prime Minister Recep Tayyip Erdogan. Again, 'the literary', even as practised by the conservative neofascist Yeats (national liberation is not a revolution). The supplementation that comes, introducing the element of the incalculable, takes us beyond nostalgic interventionist politics.

Byzantium will not be subdued by the repeated localization of the East–West chiasmus. For Orpheus, the Byzant before the letter, as Rilke taught us, only in the double kingdom did the voices become eternal and could be, imperfectly, mimed on Earth. In German, the more abstract word 'determine' is, literally, 'attuning': *die Bestimmung*, with *Stimme* in it, as in *die Stimmen*—'voices', in Rilke's lines, in *The Sonnets to Orpheus*:

---

12 Ahmet Davutoğlu, interview by Scott MacLeod, *Cairo Review of Global Affairs*, 12 March 2012. Available at: http://www.aucegypt.edu/gapp/cairoreview/pages/articleDetails.aspx?aid=143 (last accessed on 18 April 2014).

Erst in dem Doppelbereich
werden die Stimmen
ewig und mild.

Only where those two worlds join
are there pure voices,
calm, without age.[13]

Thrace predetermines Byzantium into a *mise en abyme*,
double standing in for indefinite, mirroring as in a hall of
mirrors, poetry's response to a linear sense of strife in history.
Double also as in double bind. Byzantium shows up the double bind of history as the site of struggle, the warp and woof
of the text of time, as the shuttle rises and falls. It is the double bind of democracy that confronts the modern Byzantium,
the double bind of ipseity (myself) and alterity (the other), of
the unconscious pulling away at the voting ego. It is the problem of supplementing vanguardism, supplementing the
shortfall of the unquestioned need for vanguardism.

When a great change is made in politics and economics
(national liberation is not a revolution), as time presses with
increasing opposition from all sides, it is not possible to
become completely non-vanguardist. Gramsci sitting in jail
understood that. Unless vanguardism is supplemented by
the instrumentalization of the intellectual to produce the subaltern proletarian intellectual, nothing will survive; because
people as a whole do not change epistemically as a result of

13 Rainer Maria Rilke, 'I, 9' in *The Sonnets to Orpheus* (Leslie Norris and Alan
Keele trans) (Columbia, SC: Camden House, 1989), p. 9.

the vanguardist 'revolution'. Where Gramsci was thinking of the underclass, I am thinking of ourselves, generally middle-class teachers of English literature at elite universities in India, the 'world's largest democracy', to quote CNN.

How does a robust borderlessness, preserving borders with care for people rather than capital, supplement? With a sensibility aggressively trained into suspending self-interest in the other's text—verbal, visual, oral, social. This is a training for the will to social justice, though not necessarily so. It is not a literary training alone that can do this, but when short-term solutions of regulating borderless capital—an example here is the Tobin tax proposed by the World Social Forum—call for the will to impose such a tax on oneself, we need to depend on the low-speed, long-term build-up of what I call a literary sensibility: imaginative training for epistemological performance so that an economically just world can be sustained by each generation being trained in the will specifically to social justice.

This is undoubtedly a utopian vision. I wrote it as a teacher, with full civil rights in India and nowhere else, given that the world is still not postnational, addressing the students of English, again with full civil rights in India alone, urging them to understand that utopia does not happen and yet to understand, also, their importance to the nation and the world. Indeed, I know how hard it is to sustain such a spirit in the midst of a hostile polity, but I urge the students to consider the challenge. It is in view of that impossible utopia that I understand as the task of the student and teacher of literature here and everywhere, in a world where literature is trivialized, and I quote again that passage in Benjamin: 'The past can be seized only as an image which flashes up at the instant of its recognizability, never to be seen again. [. . .] History is the object of a construction, whose site forms not with homogeneous empty time, but time filled with the now time.'

I began with borders in my childhood, youth and the present as Indian. Partition, the McMahon Line. I moved into the performative contradictions of an Indian comparative literature, relating it to the performative contradictions of global capital: a borderlessness that must preserve borders—the tradition of English-in-India being put to work for regional languages. I proposed a supplementary relationship between the two, 'the literary' introducing the dangerous element of the incalculable. I offered a reading of Yeats within the narrative of Byzantium, relating it again to the current Turkey–Greece minuet. Throughout, I insisted that a training of the imagination for literary reading produces a flexible epistemology that can, perhaps, keep saving our world.

QUESTIONS[14]

1. The Meaning of 'Organic Intellectuals of Capitalism' (Gramsci)

Most people seem to think that 'organic intellectuals' is a word or phrase of praise, meaning something like a public intellectual, or an activist intellectual. In Gramsci, the only example

[14] Since this was a lecture series, we have edited the questions and answers as they contributed to the enhancement of the general argument.

you have of an 'organic intellectual' is the organic intellectual of capitalism. There, 'organ' is not, as in Coleridge, trees and plants and organs and so on. It is more an adjective emerging from 'organization'. What he means by this term is an intellectual produced according to the social relations of force that operate a certain mode of production. I was actually trying in a sense to create a fable of this: that finance capitalism, which is the major thing of capitalist globalization, is borderlessness that must keep borders intact—a bad thing.

Comparative literature of Indian languages, which will be a borderlessness (English studies) keeping borders intact— a good thing. So, I was in effect saying that the organic intellectual I am describing, who is produced by the organization of finance capital, without deliberate intervention, can affirmatively sabotage the structure which s/he can imperfectly deduce by studying the polity as text. My conclusion: in a country as linguistically rich as ours, this other sort of borderlessness that we have in English studies can work at carefully preserving linguistic borders even as we make them permeable.

2. Rearing

I use this word to get to a place that is less restricted than what is covered by the word 'education'. This also allows me to bring in the broader scope of cultural instruction. Primo Levi, the Italian who was in Auschwitz, escaped when the Soviets came and liberated Germany after the Second World War. He was asked, 'What were those monsters like who tortured you?'[15] And what Levi said was, in effect: 'Apart from a few who really were monstrous, most of these people were really like you and me, but badly reared.'[16] In the face of the kind of dehumanizing torture in the concentration camps recorded in his book *The Drowned and the Saved* (1986), for Levi to be able to answer this brings me back to the fact that Dante allowed him to survive. I meant that through cultural and, one hopes, institutional literary training, we may be given habits that deeply relate to others first, the very principle of social justice. Unfortunately, cultural instruction is deeply gender- and class-compromised. 'Culture' is so quickly becoming a divisive word these days that I would rather say 'social permission'.

When I actually teach at Columbia and teach for training at the rural schools, I try to develop intuitions of democracy in the method of teaching, rather than talk to them about

15 'Monsters exist, but they are too few in numbers to be truly dangerous. More dangerous are [. . .] the functionaries ready to believe and act without asking questions' (Primo Levi, *Survival in Auschwitz, and The Reawakening* [Stuart Woolf trans.] [New York: Summit Books, 1986], p. 394).

16 'Coltivati male': Levi writes, 'Infatti, l'uomo incolto (e i tedeschi di Hitler, e le SS in specie, erano paurosamente incolti: non erano stati "coltivati", o erano stati coltivati male) non sa distinguere nettamente fra chi non capisce la sua lingua e chi non capisce *tout court*' ('Comunicare' in *I Sommersi E I Salvati* [Torino: Einuadi, 2007(1986)], p. 71). Raymond Rosenthal's translation: 'In fact, an uncultivated man (and Hitler's Germans, and the SS in particular, were frightfully uncultivated; they had not been "cultivated", or had been badly cultivated) does not know how to distinguish clearly between those who do not understand his language and those who do not understand *tout court*' ('Communicating' in *The Drowned and the Saved* [London: Michael Joseph, 1988], p. 71).

what they already know, that the ruling class is very cruel, absurd and so on. My subaltern teachers and students have mostly never seen white people where my schools are, and they do not connect to the America part of my existence. It is the fact that I am arriving from Calcutta which makes me their class enemy. What I try is to devise a philosophy of education that will at the same time keep alive the competitive intuition which is necessary in class struggle, or in the citizen demanding that the abstract structures of the state work for her or him, and yet keep alive other-directedness—the shuttle between ipseity and alterity. These are elementary schools and this kind of attempt becomes a part of rearing.

3. The Female Body

It is a borderline, isn't it? All bodies, in fact, are borderlines. I was not just saying 'respecting' borders, I was saying 'attending to' borders. But in the simplest possible sense, the female body is seen as permeable. It is seen as permeable in perhaps the most basic gesture of violence. To respect the border of the seemingly permeable female body, which seems to be in the benign service of humanity itself, to understand that one must attend to this border and respect it—surely this is where you and I would agree. But this is long-term preparation for thinking, not short-term implementation of solutions by those who can think.

In terms of this, the short-term work is law: changing and implementing. The long-term work is the work that I was talking about. I am glad that you picked up on that, because this borderlessness attends to borders—not just respects them, but attends to them. After all, to be borderless is also a pleasure for the female and the male—to be borderless, to be permeable, can be a pleasure. So it is attending to borders rather than simply respecting them, in that particular situation.

Also, there comes a moment when one begins to talk about gendering. One is very careful about violence, because violence can be connected to desire. So where are you going to turn the ethical into merely the moral? This is a place where, because of the incalculable, I think the idea of attending to (hypercathexis in Freud is 'attending'—not just occupying with desire, but 'hyper'. *Attendre* in French is 'to wait', so 'to wait upon') borders is very important. That is where I would go: law, training, attending to borders.

FANON READING HEGEL

I. CLAIMING

The Antilles are still not postcolonial. They are *départements et territoires d'outre-mer*—DOM-TOM. If you want to go there, you get a visa that looks exactly like a French visa. But it does not take you into the hexagon. It does not take you into France. In the context of French imperialism, neither Algeria nor, indeed, Vietnam has the same political being as the West Indies do.

Frantz Fanon writes from Algeria, not his place of origin —Martinique—when he is talking to us about Africa. A gentleman, traumatized by not being recognized as a French gentleman in France, wanting to go to a French-speaking African country—first choice: Senegal. But Léopold Sédar Senghor does not respond to him. Therefore, Fanon goes to his second choice: Algeria. The relationship with Algeria is marked by this narrative.

In the class, Spivak's remarks were preceded by presentations by Archana Joshi, PhD student at the Deparment of English, University of Pune, and Rajan Joseph Barrett, lecturer in the Department of English, University of Baroda. These papers are available upon request.

We are looking here at not Africa as a whole but at French-speaking Africa. Reading now Aimé Césaire's play *Une saison au Congo* (1966), one realizes that pan-Africanism chose the borderlessness of the imperial language to forge itself internationally. My idea of instrumentalizing English studies in India as 'borderless' in the Introduction has something like a relationship with this period. You get a sense of this in Ngugi wa Thiong'o's book *Globalectics* (2012). This is something that escaped the South Asia–focused postcolonial theory that was developed in the United States in the 1980s.

Alain Locke's book *The New Negro* is a comment on the Harlem Renaissance from within. It was published the year Fanon was born: 1925. It looked towards W. E. B. Du Bois as an older figure, a mature voice. The collection itself is full of primitivism towards African art, written by African Americans. However, Du Bois writes a piece called 'The Negro Mind Reaches Out'[1] in which he distinguishes between different kinds of colonization: the Shadow of France, the Shadow of Portugal, the Shadow of Belgium, the Shadow of Britain and the Shadow of Shadows, which is the United States—slavery. There is a difference between chattel slavery and colonialism. He discusses this even as he establishes connections.

At the Schomburg Center for Research in Black Culture of the New York Public Library there is a recording of a conversation among George Padmore, C. L. R. James and

---

1 W. E. B. Du Bois, 'The Negro Mind Reaches Out' in Alain Locke (ed.), *The New Negro: Voices of the Harlem Renaissance* (New York: Atheneum, 1992), pp. 385–414.

W. E. B. Du Bois which discusses Fanon without the Sartrean hagiography. They speak of the fact that in the Shadow of France, it was possible for the black European to be recognized as such; in other words, it is easier to be a resisting intellectual. Chapter Five of *Black Skin, White Masks*, literally, 'The Lived Experience of the Black Man' ('L'expérience vécue du Noir'), is the chapter usually suggested for reading when a selection is made.[2] I would like to suggest that this is the chapter, right in the middle of the book, where Fanon takes leave of negritude, which may be too sentimental. He moves from that space into something else. That is Chapter Seven, 'The Negro and Recognition', the last chapter of the book, where Fanon reads Hegel. The first words of this chapter are interesting: that the problem with Alfred Adler is that he is looking at the individual, whereas we have to look at the social. This is also an indirect statement on the intellectual's obligation to move from mere lived experience. Fanon thus distinguishes himself from Adler, and that is the distinction for himself from negritude, which does not consider class.

It is interesting that when he talks about with whom the Martinican compares himself, it is not the white man, not the father, not the boss, not god, but someone like himself, his own counterpart under the patronage of the white man.

2 In Chapter 5 of Frantz Fanon, *Black Skin, White Masks* (Charles Lam Markmann trans.) (London: Pluto Press, 2008 [1986]), the word *Nègre* is always translated as 'Black Man'. I believe it loses something in the translation, especially since we are talking about a lived experience. 'Nigger' would be too strong. This is the kind of distance which translation cannot traverse, and comparative literature must emphasize through its absolute requirement for linguistic proficiency.

I repeat that it is absolutely important that Fanon is pointing to the successful diasporic of colour. We have to bear it in mind when we consider the situation today in the global South, including India, across the spectrum from literary education to foreign direct investment.

Helped by this conviction, Fanon puts himself in the place of the Hegelian Subject, clear away from the well-placed diasporic. This is of course neither master nor slave which, reduced to 'slave is black, master is white' (he says a little bit of that too), would not take into account that the master–slave dialectic is simply a 'moment' of the entire text of *The Phenomenology of Spirit* (1807), which describes the trajectory of the Subject as such. That is the amazing thing about Fanon as a reader. He appropriates and claims the Hegelian text so that the Subject in Hegel is what Fanon inhabits, in order to turn the text round. Fanon is reading, not just giving a commentary on Hegel.

How does one read? One inserts oneself inside the text of the other, not as her/himself. It is not 'Please Hegel, be like me!' It is rather 'Hegel, here I come, to ventriloquize you.' It is to act out the text as the text of the other, the enemy's text. In Hegel, as we know, it is an epistemograph, a kind of graphic presentation of the episteme moving from Absolute Necessity to Absolute Knowledge. Within this, the master–slave dialectic marks the moment of the emergence of reason.

Thus, the master–slave dialectic is not just the historical story of masters and slaves to describe the transition from feudalism to capitalism. Fanon is not a philosopher. Fanon is an activist, and of course also a psychiatrist. Additionally, Fanon is reading a very powerful French translation of Hegel, by Jean Hyppolite, who undoubtedly marks Hegel's German classical philosophy with his own post-existentialist spirit. Fanon has found excellent translators but even then there are problems.

What does Fanon want to claim from Hegel? That in order for the Subject to be a Subject, he must be ready to die (Fanon is speaking of the male). If you read it carefully like an activist psychiatrist who is engaged in fighting hard, you will see that he is not just giving the somewhat banal description of what happens between the master and the slave. Almost at the time that he is writing Chapter Seven, the French government puts a ban on him. He has to leave Algeria. So Fanon moves, first to Tunis, and then, when he is diagnosed with acute leukaemia, into hospital. (*The Wretched of the Earth* [1961] was dictated in 10 weeks, during this last illness.) He is going into hospital but his very existence there is banned by the French. Some Italian reporters are told his room number in the hospital. Fanon says: 'My god, are you crazy, do you want to kill me? Move me.' And it is true: that room is blown up a couple of hours later.

So when we are talking about this man reading Hegel, we are not just talking about someone who is giving a narrative description of Hegel's discourse. This idea—you must be ready to die—is a different idea because he did not know yet about his illness. And here, we must remember that *Herr*—translated 'master' in the master–slave dialectic—is also the Lord God and his son Jesus. Hegel is on the way to the transformation of religion into philosophy.

If we read the paragraphs that come before the master–slave dialectic, we see that it is definitely not just a psychologized story of masters and slaves. Hegel is talking about the emergence of *Bewusstsein*, which is a depersonalized phenomenal Being-conscious, which will emerge into the clear light of reason only in the next chapter. He therefore has to come to a moment when this Being-conscious—this *Bewusstsein*—has to emerge, somehow, with no element of anything conscious in the Subject at all. This is a fantastic task. Philosophy here is like crazed poetry of very high order. You cannot 'apply' this attempt to do an emergence of consciousness from something that is completely unlike consciousness. How will mind emerge?

Let us focus on the word *Bewusstsein*. Before the emergence of this word, all of the nouns working towards it end in -*heit*; such as *Gewissheit*, certainty. *Heit* is not 'being', but '-ness'. *Sein* is '-being'. In those paragraphs, Hegel is moving from -*heit* words to -*sein* words, without touching the heavy -*heit* word—*Wahrheit*, 'truth'. The first word is certitude, *Gewissheit*, without doubt. Correct facts. And then, *Wahrheit*, a -*heit* word which has the weight of an unattached consciousness, truth hanging out on its own.

Preparing to give this series of lectures, I was rereading this part of the *Phenomenology*. This section reminded me strongly of *Anti-Oedipus* (1983) and there are indeed very strong affinities. Hegel is talking about desire—*die Begierde*—'the desired', again, an impersonal abstraction; and so are Gilles Deleuze and Félix Guattari, the writers of *Anti-Oedipus*. Here we must also place the Jacques Lacan of 'The Subversion of the Subject and the Dialectic of Desire in the Freudian Unconscious', the 'poet'-psychoanalyst who locates in Hegel a metonym of his account of the transformation of non-specular, non-Subject-ed Desire into a Subject-controlled Desire by the workings of fantasy.[3]

For the English translation of *Anti-Oedipus*, Foucault protests too much, warning the reader, '*Anti-Oedipus* is not flashy Hegel.'[4] Of course, more or less an admission that this is Hegel flashing up.

Towards the end of the master–slave dialectic, precisely where Hegel is talking about absolute fear and the acceptance of death, Hegel also says that if this is empiricized into actual examples of resistance, we will fall out of the philosophical project, short-circuiting it in the empirical. Is Fanon making a mistake? Let us consider a genealogy and go back to Gramsci, who, when he wrote about the 'new intellectual' in the *Prison Notebooks* (1929–35), said that he must be in the master–disciple relationship.[5]

The intellectual, then, is the disciple, and the master is the socioeconomic environment. Gramsci also de-routes the

3 Jacques Lacan, 'The Subversion of the Subject and the Dialectic of Desire in the Freudian Unconscious' in *Écrits: A Selection* (Alan Sheridan trans.) (London: Routledge, 2001), pp. 323–60.

4 Michel Foucault, preface to Gilles Deleuze and Félix Guattari, *Anti-Oedipus: Capitalism and Schizophrenia* (Robert Hurley, Mark Seem, and Helen R. Lane trans) (Minneapolis: University of Minnesota Press, 1983), pp. *xi–xiv*; here, p. *xiv*.

5 Antonio Gramsci, 'On Education' in *Selections From The Prison Notebooks* (Quintin Hoare and Geoffrey Nowell Smith eds and trans) (London: Lawrence and Wishart, 1971), pp. 26–43.

Hegelian *Phenomenology*, displaces the slave into the 'disciple', moves him to the chapter on 'Reason', fracturing the Subject into intellectual-subaltern. To learn how to access the subaltern, there will be a reversal of the master–slave relationship, where the intellectual is the slave, displaced into master–disciple. Gramsci is psychologizing, or rather, epistemologizing—doing things that are not correct with the philosophical text. Fanon uses a descriptive text as an activist text, in order to turn around. Gramsci is using a descriptive text to describe an activist methodology of an epistemologically transformative kind.

So are these mistakes? Was Martin Luther King just making a mistake about Gandhi? These kinds of 'mistakes' (Sanil V., from the Department of Humanities and Social Science, Indian Institute of Technology, Delhi, has theorized my notion of 'intended mistake' in an instructive fashion)[6] are proofs of the most engaged ways of reading, claiming the text as the other's text for me, and we ought to look at the 'mistakes' in that spirit. The specialists will stop you. Someone who really knows Hegel will say, 'Ah!' But in fact, these mistakes tell us something about what to do with philosophy. The mistake that was made with Marx's philosophy was—thanks to Engels, who did not understand Marx's counter-intuitive genius—to use it as if it were a blueprint for unmediated imitation in statecraft. That is the exact opposite of 'claiming the text' by entering its protocols. Let us guard these examples of Gramsci, of Fanon, of Martin Luther King, as engaged readings producing a map of 'mistakes'.

QUESTIONS

1. Gramsci and the Organic Intellectual

One must not find refuge in placing oneself in Gramsci's 'everybody', in his statement that everybody is an intellectual, and thus avoid academic homework. To find the everybody who is an intellectual, I would travel to my schools for the children of the landless illiterate. Indeed, they can think, but they do not resemble the 'everybody'-ist students at elite universities. Every self-description of the intellectual elite as 'everybody' is an interested declaration. I should also mention that Gramsci does not have any section called 'Intellectuals' in his *Prison Notebooks*. What was put together as such a section by Gramsci's executor Palmyro Togliatti exists in the *Notebooks* as scattered passages on education. There is a section in Gramsci where he is talking about how to produce permanent structures out of what Croce calls 'political passion'. He speculates in one short paragraph ending with 'etc.', giving the title 'Passions' to this paragraph in the middle of a section on Machiavelli. The present English translators shift this speculative paragraph into a sustained argument about education, without any critical notice.

Therefore, when we are talking about Gramsci talking about intellectuals, let us pay him the respect of researching the continuity of the text. This unjustly imprisoned young intellectual is trying to write down his own speculations, which will perhaps become a book in the future. (In the event, he died before this could happen.) It is an open text written in bits of uneven length in different cardboard note-books. The idea about everybody being an intellectual came to him on a day when he was thinking about how to distinguish between common sense and good sense.

Let me add that the claim to subalternity—a feature of thinking of oneself as everybody—is pretty common among metropolitan radicals. To such folks I always say, 'Do not look above, but look below to see the ways in which you are distinguished from these lower reaches.' Let us not abdicate the responsibility of being trained intellectuals. We do not think in the way in which people deprived of the right to intellectual labour think.

My example of the everybody who can think is an exceptional subaltern: my associate Nimai Lohar in Birbhum, who is a completely illiterate and innumerate person. I do not think illiteracy is a good thing but the really intelligent illiterate are ruined by the bad education available in subalternity. For them, it is a tragic fact that remaining illiterate has protected their intelligence. In Purulia, there was Tulu Shabor. These are people who really do think, but it would be hopelessly romantic to think that they are Gramscian philosophers.

Sunil Lohar, the person who runs the ecological agricultural part of the project has had only four years of schooling. That is also a person who thinks. That is not to be compared to a self-styled non-intellectual. Gramsci did not write for students of university that everybody can think. He wrote for those members of the proletariat and the subaltern classes who were, I repeat, denied the right to intellectual labour.

I tried to narrativize this argument to my co-workers there by emphasizing *matha khatano*—making the head work—which is the prerogative of the ruling classes, whereas *gator khatano*—making the body work—remains the obligation of the worker and the SC/ST.[7] The way of teaching there is comparable to the way of teaching at Columbia because the superpower children, full of pride at helping and empowering, do not engage in intellectual self-analytical labour, which I am urging you to undertake as well, and need to have their desire for subalternity rearranged just as much.

In this area, Fanon is wrong, generalizing from the Martinican upper class about essentialized categories called 'the colonized' and 'the colonizer' as he inhabits a country which is not his own, working tirelessly.

The real problem is that even the very smart ones, because of this kind of cognitive and epistemic violence as well as ideological production, accept their wretchedness as normal and know of no resistance that is not simply suicidal violence. This is why subalternist South Asian historians talked about subaltern classes who brought their subalternity to crisis. This is why you must not indulge in self-selected wretchedness: How will I be the lowest common denominator in Gramsci's text? These people do not have access to the borderlessness of English! As I said, they have never seen

7 Scheduled Castes and Scheduled Tribes, recognized in the Constitution of India as historically disadvantaged groups.

white people, except one person who is a party hack. He saw them inside Santiniketan—the Tagore university.

2. Reclaiming Philosophy in Postcoloniality

Why is there this unending focus on theology as philosophy in the non-philosophical literary, generally with English Department postcolonialists in India? We have, after all, a tremendous tradition of rational critique. It seems to me that this ought to be reclaimed and not just remain part of Philosophy Departments. To earn the right to reclaim is without guarantees. It is easily said: 'I am reclaiming.' I think it is best to do the reading as carefully as possible, without the desire to reclaim. Perhaps people in other parts of the world, some perhaps illiterate, some not recognized, have thought this, but I have encountered it in Aristotle, where he says all you can do is careful mimesis, and poesis will emerge out of *tuché* (chance).

Assia Djebar told me once, 'None of the Algerians are going to like my stuff on Carthage because I like Polybius. You're not supposed to like the enemy.' In the beginning of *Fantasia* (1993), she is trying to get into the head of the French captain as he is looking towards Algiers, as the ship approaches land.[8] Kamal Majumdar in his book *Antarjali Jatra* (1962) pretty much asks, 'How is it that our ancestors accepted sati? They were human beings, as indeed am I.'[9]

8 Assia Djebar, *Fantasia: An Algerian Cavalcade* (Dorothy S. Blair trans.) (London: Heinemann Educational Books, 1993).

9 Kamalkumar Majumdar, *Antarjali Jatra* (Calcutta: Subarnarekha, 1981).

This mysteriousness of history is a much more interesting way to reclaim than going in thinking of oneself as a big-deal reclaimer. We go in with humility to read as the text wants to be read and then slowly, if we have learnt well enough, the text begins to turn. Let other people notice that we are reclaiming, if we are.

II. READING

The idea of reading everything in English translation here makes me, as a comparativist, a little melancholy. If I asked you to remember that Fanon the Martinican is reading Hegel through the translation by Jean Hyppolite, how can I reconcile myself to the fact that you are reading Fanon in English translation? If I say the idea of India is a little bit different from the idea of the Antilles, again, how can I reconcile it with your inability to reach it through French? Maryse Condé wrote a novel in the 1970s called *Heremakhonon*, which confronts the situation, not only of French and English but of the many languages in the African context absent in the Antilles. A single-language place like yours (English and your mother tongue) cannot understand the language borders that keep the African everyday alive. Condé allows us to think that in going towards French-speaking Africa, Fanon is perhaps looking for what she will call 'Niggers with ancestors'.[10] How shall we understand it when, living in this many-languaged

---

10 Maryse Condé, *Heremakhonon: A Novel* (Richard Philcox trans.) (Boulder, CO: Lynne Rienner, 1982).

place (although not to be compared with Africa's wealth of languages), we have chosen to ignore it?

I will leave these questions unanswered. But as we move into the second session of Fanon and Hegel, I will simply remind us that we must not psychologize Hegel and we must not think that 'Black' remains an important category in Fanon. Fanon is interested not in individuals but in the environment. This fits in with Hegel's epistemographic work—a picture of the Subject moving, a philosophical principle on the move. Yet, the de Manian insight that the *Phenomenology* is an autobiographical novel hints that Hegel is himself fighting the tendency and the desire to make it a psychological storyline. Hegel is trying to remain a philosopher. That is the conflict.

This relates to Fanon's insistence that it is not the individual but the collective that we should think about. What Fanon is against is narcissism. Narcissism for a psychologist-psychiatrist is a different kind of word from what it is for us. Narcissus to Oedipus is the storyline in normative psychology. Our homegrown psychology specialists, Sudhir Kakar and V. S. Naipaul, both diagnose India by suggesting that Indian men have not graduated from Narcissus into Oedipus.[11]

So what do we know about Narcissus from Ovid? Narcissus looks into the water and falls in love with his own

11 See Sudhir Kakar, *The Inner World: A Psychoanalytic Study of Childhood and Society* (Delhi: Oxford University Press India, 1978) and V. S. Naipaul, *The Mimic Men* (London: Penguin, 1987[1967]). Naipaul modifies his position in his *India: A Million Mutinies Now* (London: Heinemann, 1990).

image. Teiresias tells Narcissus' mother, Liriope, that Narcissus will live to old age 'so long as he never knows himself'.[12] Narcissus says: I do not care, *Iste ego sum*. The sentence here is both 'it I am'—a hetero-tautology. In Latin, the single sentence that Narcissus utters shows the "is" suppressed. And in this hetero-tautology, the difference between the 'am' and the 'is' in the same sentence, rises the history of the Subject in Hegel and, in the master–slave dialectic—the transition from feudalism into capitalism, self-consciousness blossoming into reason—Hegel carefully puts that mark of where the *ego* over-balances the *iste*. You move from Narcissus into Oedipus, because Narcissus can only utter the hetero-tautology, whereas Oedipus, punished, symptomatic, can say just *ego sum*.

On the Oedipal scene, one is not in love with one's own image, not the Subject of a hetero-tautology, 'I am it; it is I.'[13] Teiresias is male and female. A male and female person cannot teach Narcissus not to be Narcissus. Therefore, in the

---

12 Ovid, 'Narcissus and Echo' in *Metamorphoses* (David Raeburn trans.) (London: Penguin, 2004), 3.348.109.

13 This is, of course, language-bound. It is not possible in a language where you do not have these verbal distinctions. If we were really talking about the phenomenology of human beings in general, we would have to translate in all the languages of the world this scene of the initiation of the man into law and let that remain as a warning scene for the comparativist, that this particular thing, easy in the Indo-European languages, has to be teased out in some other way for the users of other languages, and language does not come before mind. I am going to lay aside that task of entering the 'lingual memory' of other languages, the signature task of the comparativist, and continue to argue as if that is easily denied. From now on, therefore, my argument is limited, although it cannot say so.

sexual-difference mythology of the Greeks, which we think of as commanding human pathology as such. (Having put the task of lingual memory to sleep, we think that the man in love with the mirror image cannot be rescued by any vision of AC/DC as sexual equality.) The hetero-tautology bursts forth with the non-subjected epistemograph until Oedipus can say, 'I am I, am I,' and, 'All creation shivers / With that sweet cry.'[14] 'I am I' inaugurates a better history: 'I carry my father's name.' Let us remember that this is not only a gender-fixed history but also a class-fixed one—and again, all the cultures of the world cannot assume this patronymic history. The basic idea in the early work of Kakar and Naipaul, then, is that the colonized male is so in love with his own image that he cannot graduate into becoming the carrier of his patronymic, because he is owned by others. Fanon wants to break that individualistic judgement and invokes the collective.

Here is *Black Skin, White Masks*: 'I know doctors and dentists, however, who continue to throw at each other diagnostic mistakes that were made fifteen years ago. [. . .] One of the traits of the Antillean is his desire to dominate the other. [. . .] The Other comes on stage as a kind of fixture; the hero (that's me).'[15] Fanon is giving us Hegel's description of the Subject stuck in the first stage—notice. We are going to get to master and slave but keep this one in mind. When Fanon is starting, 'The Black Man and Hegel', he is actually

14 W. B. Yeats, 'He and She' in *Collected Poems of W. B. Yeats* (London: Collector's Library, 2010), p. 383.

15 Fanon, *Black Skin, White Masks*, p. 164, translation modified.

using Hegel. If he is coming to Hegel via a rejection of mere negritude, he is also not prepared to take Hegel's descriptive posture at face value.

'*No* to scorn of man. *No* to degradation of man. *No* to exploitation of man. *No* to the butchery of what is most human in man: freedom,' Fanon writes. 'The self takes its place by opposing itself, Fichte said. Yes and no. [. . .] *Yes* to life. *Yes* to love. *Yes* to generosity.'[16] If Hegel descriptively works through negations and sublations, Fanon deliberately makes a mistake, saying that he is not going to be just negating on his way to sublation and he is not going to take Hegel as a description of what happens.

In the beginning, the hero—the Subject as object or other—comes on stage as a kind of fixture. Fanon does not mention Freud at all but, as a psychiatrist, he mentions Adler. Unlike Lacan, who understands Hegel's and Descartes's metonymic relationship to psychoanalysis, Fanon looks at psychology and psychiatry and says that the Hegelian description does not take into account that there are three terms for the Martinican in the Antillean comparison. If the Adlerian comparison comprises two terms, polarized by the ego, the Antillean comparison is stopped by a third term: its governing fiction. The word 'fiction' here does not relate to personal experience but to social evaluation. And this is what he explodes. As he advances the Antillean situation, rather than the European diagnostic situation, he goes by way of a governing fiction rather than by way of the real answer.

16 Ibid., p. 173.

So look into yourselves: when you actually decide that you are positing the truth about things, whereas they (whoever they are) do not really know anything, look also at this smart young man who gave his life to his work (although he did not die in the field) and whose work has lasted long enough that we who are over 70 are still getting wisdom from a man who died at 36. In order to be able to be wise in that way: every time you are obliged to utter that disgraceful remark to people like me, abroad, who are cruelly patronized by the white man, 'Ah, this is India,' remember that Fanon would not allow that. Fanon is able to see, on both sides— the European mistake and the Antillean suggestion of invincible uniqueness. There are competing and governing fictions. This is what gives him his power and this is what makes him useful. Otherwise, he would be just someone who resembles us. He does not resemble us. We should be able to earn the right to enter, as readers, this unusual double intuition, rather than take Fanon simply as the model of the 'African' revolution or assume that he is describing the postcolonial predicament. He is doing something more: he is combating governing fictions.

He comes back and he says: 'I am Narcissus, and I want to see reflected in the eyes of the other an image of myself that satisfies me.'[17] When Kakar and Naipaul say that you are stuck in Narcissus, remember Fanon turning Narcissus around. People mostly have nothing to say about the woman in the Narcissus story: Echo. 'I am Echo, and I want to see

17 Ibid., p. 165, translation modified.

reflected in the eyes of the other an image of myself that satisfies me.'

As a result, in Martinique, there is the man at the top, and there are his courtiers, the indifferent and the humiliated. Every day, one sees this kind of situation replicated, even at the university, and not only in India. There are different ways: a little bit of fawning, how long you keep someone waiting. Do not just think you are reading Fanon. Ask yourself, 'Is this text describing my environment?' Be as honest as you can be: 'Is this text describing the life I live and in which I participate? I want to be the man at the top so that there are courtiers fawning and opening my door.' This is a sign of weakness, and something that Fanon is criticizing. I do not necessarily believe in all this weakness/strength talk, but that is the analysis here.

Fanon goes on to say that Martinicans are hungry for reassurance; and he suggests that now that we have found the Adlerian line of orientation of the Antillean, we have to look for its origin. Fanon writes as a diagnostic psychiatrist, not as a literary person. Although he is able to recognize fiction, his definition of fiction is close to the opposite of truth. We have to remember that during this time, Fanon is writing his dissertation, which is occupying his mind. He is a gnoseological psychiatrist writing a dissertation for doctoral validation. We cannot forget this. His dissertation is dry, full of data, going from data to conclusion, written for a future that never happened. This is the person who is going to Adler and saying, 'We must look for its origin.' This, therefore, is an etiology;

the Black Man belongs to an inferior race; he tries to resemble the superior race. The Martinican compares himself not to the white man/father/boss/god but his own counterpart under the patronage of the white man.

Where does he get some proof of this? Literature becomes evidence for him. *El Valiente Negro en Flandes* (published in 1638) by Andrés de Claramonte, the contemporary of Lope de Vega, is where he finds proof. Many of our dissertations are ruined by the discussion of one piece of literature as evidence for an entire sociological generalization. This is why, and rightly so, we are not taken seriously by the qualitative social scientists, because we treat literature as evidence, thereby demeaning both literature and ourselves, and then we decide that on the basis of one piece of literature, you can draw a conclusion. But when a mind doctor does it, they are doing something different. Freud says in 'The Uncanny' (1919) that he can find in literature evidence of the sort that he cannot find in real life.[18] This is why he turns towards literature. This is why literature has been called 'an experience of the impossible'. What you are seeing here is not proof of what Fanon says but the idea that the literary is in fact giving you an evidence that it is not possible for you to experience so cleanly in 'real life'.

---

18 Sigmund Freud, 'The Uncanny' in *The Standard Edition of the Complete Psychological Works of Sigmund Freud* (James Strachey ed.), VOL. 17, *From the History of an Infantile Neurosis* (James Strachey with Anna Freud, Alix Strachey and Alan Tyson trans) (London: Hogarth, 1955), pp. 217–56; here, p. 250.

Freud gives us this insight. Fanon, trying to decide how to understand himself beyond the notion of mere race and his own country, finds in this European text the representation of a Black Man who says something that he believes is true. That is not the way we should read literature, if we are literary folk. We should cut Fanon a little slack here when he reads literature as evidence, understand that he is reading the text as mind, as he would in his practice read minds as text. We cannot imitate him absolutely. The mind doctor does it one-on-one, not just in groups, and therefore when Fanon says that it is not just individual but social, we have to believe him more. What I am trying to do is to talk about subject position. And when he reads literature as evidence, we have to understand his protocols and not imitate him, as socialism attempted to imitate Marx.

It is Fanon's subject position that, as a trained gnoseological psychiatrist, his disciplinary production is epistemologically different from ours, and it is our obligation to honour that.

Enabled by this evidentiary reading of fiction, he can contradict Octave Mannoni and suggest to the friend who has 'fulfilled in a dream his wish to become white' that 'The environment, society are responsible for your delusion.' This would mean undoing a self-signification—'[T]he place that has been assigned to you'.[19] For philosophically trained, highly educated French people to say 'assigned' will come to mean the fiction of a 'subject position'. 'Assigned' means in

19 Fanon, *Black Skin, White Masks*, p. 168.

a structure which makes meaning. 'Signification' means making into a sign, assigning. Signification does not just mean meaning. It is this assign-system that Fanon will undo.

'If I were an Adlerian'. By the end of the chapter, Fanon will show us that not only is he a Hegelian but he is, in fact, the appropriate Hegelian because he knows how to say no to the system. He is, in other words, entering and using, entering and using: affirmative sabotage. To say no from the outside is to lose this extraordinary machine, Hegel's thinking. He says: 'If I were an Adlerian', I would say I believe that you should agree to remain in the place assigned to you.[20] What the French will call 'assigning', the Germans—in the structural picture—called a *Verhältnis*. When a Marx, a Hegel, a Kant, use the word *Verhältnis*, they mean the appropriate place in a structural picture, as in an epistemograph, an assigned place, as Fanon was saying. In other words, he is saying, if I were an Adlerian, I might give the kind of restricted Hegelian position: what the *Phenomenology* describes is what happens, and you better believe it because you are fixed there—it is fixed, that is your *Verhältnis*. Fanon says that he would not say that but, rather, would say that it is not the necessity of the epistemograph but the contingency of the environment that gives the assignment. The assurance of 'If you say this, the rest will follow' is the 'revolutionary' mistake that has undone socialism. There is no direct line between consciousness-raising and the will to social justice. I have been arguing that literary training may unblock that

20 Ibid., translation modified.

path, although there is no guarantee. Perhaps Kant hints at this by his use of the word 'almost'—*beinahe*—in the sentence in 'What Is Enlightenment?' (1784): '[I]f only freedom is granted, enlightenment is almost sure to follow.'[21]

Before he enters Hegel, then, Fanon is doing a Hegel before the letter. That is what this chapter is: he is doing a small-*h* Hegel, 'I am Narcissus [. . .] Me, nothing but me.' For Fanon, the Martinican is a Narcissus, the other is dead except for the task of reflecting back the self's own image to itself, and in this situation in Martinique, 'one finds the top man, the hierarchy, the indifferent.'[22] This is a dramatization or, better, a staging, a *mise en scène*, of the Hegelian philosopheme, a unit of Hegel's philosophical thinking.

Fanon's text is training the reader how to read the Hegel section. For the literary reader, most texts, even terrible texts, are a transactional space. This is how it prepares you for the ethical reflex, by making you get into the movements of the other text. The reader is not thinking 'How can I read Hegel?' or 'How can I read Fanon?' but, rather, asking, 'Where is the text taking me?' I am suspending my desire to read it in a certain poco way, in a certain feminist way, and so on. The reader holds back.

In order to read Fanon reading Hegel, you have to read Hegel carefully on your own beforehand. You cannot just read Hegel through Fanon. Then you see that Fanon is

21 Immanuel Kant, 'What Is Enlightenment?' in *Kant On History* (Lewis White Beck ed. and trans.) (New York: Macmillan, 1963), pp. 3–10; here, p. 4.
22 Fanon, *Black Skin, White Masks*, p. 165, translation modified.

pre-staging Hegel in a non-philosophical idiom before we enter the Hegel passage. All texts, I repeat, are transactional, and they teach you how to read, not just the text but also the world. The Hegel section is about recognition. And you have learnt by now to recognize the voice of Frantz Fanon in Hegel, acting out the master–slave dialectic, only if you have read the first part of Fanon's reading by suspending yourself into the text to see what it is up to. You may not recognize that it is Hegel before Hegel, but you will certainly get to the picture of this Subject, Narcissus, fixed, wanting to see the image of its own power in the eye of the other. You will see also someone who says, 'I will not take my assigned place.' If you read carefully like a literary reader with some sense of the history of the French language, and the history of German philosophy, you will be in this unfolding. This is why this idea of saying 'I am only the completely ignorant man,' as per Gramsci's notion of 'everybody' as an intellectual, is a disgraceful idea, because then we should burn the universities.

The topos of 'something will follow' is common in the thematics of the philosophy of education. Fanon writes: 'I wonder sometimes if school inspectors and departmental heads know what they are doing in the colonies. For twenty years in their school programmes, they desperately try to make a white man out of the Black Man.'[23] Fanon is really talking about primary education as well. Otherwise there is no 20 years in school. Questions about undertaking the rearrangement of desires at the adult level within people's

23 Ibid., p. 168, translation modified.

movements of course has a positive answer. But it is also true that if one starts doing it with children then one is doing a much more difficult thing, which in the long run will probably yield more results; because educating children is like writing on wet cement: when the cement hardens, the habits, one hopes, are going to be there. Therefore, the responsibility is also somewhat greater. Benjamin, in his 'Critique of Violence', writes about education as 'divine violence':

> Mythic violence is bloody power over mere life for its own sake; divine violence is pure power over all life for the sake of the living. The first demands sacrifice; the second accepts it.
>
> This divine power is not only attested by religious tradition but is also found in present-day life at least in one sanctioned manifestation. The educative power, which in its perfected form stands outside the law, is one of its manifestations. These are defined, therefore, not by miracles directly performed by God but by the expiating moment in them that strikes without bloodshed, and, finally, by the absence of all lawmaking. To this extent it is justifiable to call this violence, too, annihilating; but it is only so relatively, with regard to goods, right, life, and suchlike, never absolutely, with regard to the soul of the living.[24]

24 Walter Benjamin, 'Critique of Violence' (Edmund Jephcott trans.) in *Selected Writings*, VOL. 1, *1913–1926* (Marcus Bullock and Michael W. Jennings eds) (Cambridge, MA: Harvard University Press, 1996), pp. 236–52; here, p. 250.

Du Bois was also devoted to the idea of education, to the extent that 'the dictatorship of the proletariat' for him became intimately connected to the education of the proletariat into electorally imaginative citizenship and, as for Gramsci, as I have emphasized, his material on 'intellectuals' is actually focused on education.[25] Du Bois's masterful analysis in *Black Reconstruction* (1935) persuades the reader that the 13th, 14th and 15th Amendments introduced into the US Constitution, after a bitter struggle at the end of the American Civil War, failed because of American racism. The book is therefore chiefly about the education of the entire population and an excoriation of what he calls 'the propaganda of history'.[26] He quotes generalizations from history classes as they were taught, including a history course at Columbia University. Like Fanon, Du Bois is commenting on education as training to be a white man.

These activist intellectuals are so interested in this kind of education because it is, precisely, imaginative activism supplementing the fragility of mere reason. They are not just reading Hegel correctly or incorrectly. And today, I

25 Before Gramsci was incarcerated, he had already offered the controversial idea of Workers' Councils, a pedagogic supplement to the more organizational and systemic idea of unions and a connection between syndicality and the Party. Once in jail, with time to think, to examine how exactly the strike in Turin failed, he became completely convinced in education into parliamentarity—rather than leaving it to what used to be called 'parliamentary cretinism'.

26 W. E. B. Du Bois, *Black Reconstruction in America: Toward a History of the Part Which Black Folk Played in the Attempt to Reconstruct Democracy in America, 1860–1880* (San Diego, CA: Harcourt, Brace, 1935).

am insisting that all teachers, including literary criticism teachers, are activists of the imagination. It is not a question of just producing correct descriptions, which should of course be produced, but which can always be disproved; otherwise nobody can write dissertations. There must be, at the same time, the sense of how to train the imagination, so that it can become something other than Narcissus waiting to see his own powerful image in the eyes of the other. Such waiting or attendance, the hierarchy within universities, is a travesty of teaching, so keep this in mind. What the American 60s taught us was that you do not transform the centuries-old structure of universities by removing yourself and doing People's Alliance teach-ins. Here, too, what you need is critical intimacy, not critical distance.

Even while writing his dissertation, then, Fanon can write: 'I wonder sometimes if school inspectors and departmental heads know what they are doing in the colonies.' This is an example of the two-step I describe above. It is remarkable that Fanon does not simply fault these officials, suggesting that they are destroying the children in the colonies. He is saying that they do not know what they are doing. I want to add here that this exactly corroborates my experience in West Bengal. The state's Board of Secondary Education is well-meaning but they do not know what their efforts produce. They do not have any idea what mental furniture the lowest sector of the electorate have, what desires need uncoercive rearranging, how the use of books, related to the millenially withheld right to intellectual labour, should be made possible in the books themselves. It is not a question of individual guilt.

(It should be mentioned in this connection that, if for us students and teachers of English Honours at an elite university in India, English offers an example of sabotageable borderlessness, the preparation of a class-sensitive collectivity for carrying on this work suffers because of the problem of the sanctioned ignorance of well-intentioned 'inspectors and departmental heads'. Any extended involvement with our argument would require developing the capacity to analyse and intervene.)

If we need new textbooks, they must engage with the minds that will use them. In Tagore's exquisite textbooks, no directions are given, because he is writing for the already-inspired middle class. But Fanon knows this. This is why, I believe, before entering Hegel, he emphasizes education. I am sharing this with you to emphasize that when we read, we do so not only to produce a correct description of Hegel; we read to read.

I will go even further—venture into the dangerous element of the incalculable in supplementation. I will speculate that Fanon writes this before entering Hegel because Hegel is a white mentor, race-specific to Western Europe. I can imagine the text asking: 'Am I trying to make a white man out of myself by putting myself in the place of the Subject in Hegel?' I am emphasizing this because readers do not look at this obsession with education in Gramsci, Du Bois, Fanon and others.

What answer might the text give? 'Yes and no.' The 'no' is an unwitting legitimation by reversal. This is the moment of transgression that allows us to enter with critical intimacy and attempt to operate affirmative sabotage. We must repeat that affirmative sabotage is to change the instrument so that it can be used to undermine its felicitous end. And the 'yes' in the 'yes and no' gives us a toe-hold. The text puts us in a position, if we are reading carefully and following signals, to know what to look for when we are reading. It makes us ready to read in a certain way. Yet it is also necessary to remember that the expression or staging of a desire does not mean that the desire is fulfilled in the text. In philosophy, the statement of the problem is a hard enough task. To be able to lay out the desire so that the reader can participate in the desire is the first step. As we saw in Yeats, mistakes themselves can be staged by the text: 'Unwearied still, lover by lover, / They paddle in the cold / Companionable streams or climb the air'; but 'Upon the brimming water among the stones / Are nine-and-fifty swans.'[27] 'Nine-and-fifty swans' obviously stages a desire that will fail. Or, 'Twenty minutes more or less I was blessed and could bless'—temporal measurement interfering with the conviction of salvation and the agency of salvation. The text shows a desire but not its fulfilment. A declarative becomes a question. The reader learns to read. The reader sees what the text is preparing her/him for, and then begins reading Hegel, not just out of the Hegel book but also out of her/his entry into the textuality of an unusual writer from

27 Yeats, 'The Wild Swans At Coole', p. 187.

Martinique who was completely unlike them, who died in 1961 and who left us nothing more and nothing less than a text. This sort of training makes the muscles of the ethical reflex stronger: we have entered the textuality that is the legacy of this unusual man, we have learnt to make the reading movements dictated by his text, without the guarantee that we are correct. That is also important. When you are doing your cardio, you don't know whether you are going to have a heart attack and die tomorrow. The mind is not less important than the body. The next step is not to freeze the readings—readers who are going to become teachers! We are ready to enter Hegel.

POSTSCRIPT: GENDER

We have reminded ourselves that it is inappropriate to treat a philosopheme like a narrateme, to treat one unit of philosophizing like a story. We have suggested that this 'mistake' has been consistently made with reference to Hegel's *Phenomenology*, and in some ways, the text asks for it. Let us then make another easy intended mistake and find in Hegel's description of the emergence of another self-consciousness the moment of the abstractability of gender.

We will keep in mind that the moment of the abstractability of gender is what allows access to abstraction. It is this instrument or weapon that, in the course of the centuries, will enable the encounter with the abstract as such—capital, in the eighteenth century. It is then that the theme of women's leadership, of equality before the law, with no diversity but that of class, begins to emerge. The point here is that gender, unrecognizable as the prime mover, is now introduced as a belated item made possible by the movement of history. From now on, leadership studies—male, female or queer—is the production of a vanguard, however fragmented or particularized. As we reconcile ourselves into the complicity with benevolent sexists, learning how to fight the elite institution with its own weapons, we realize, perhaps, that we will be able to come to the aid of those fighting outside the academy, in the streets, in justified self-interest, only by providing the necessary moment of auto-critique and the protection of the class privilege that comes precisely with moving from opposition to alternative. I say 'perhaps' because the seduction of obliterating the persistent divide between the fighting vanguard and the anyone in and off the street is too great. Only if this complicity is forever acknowledged, not as tragedy but as farce, do we earn the right to call this affirmative sabotage.

It is in this spirit that we will take another look at the pages before the opening of the master–slave section in Hegel's *Phenomenology*, where Hegel prepares for that story, not looking for plot details about women or queers to imitate in self-representation, which is the usual academic liberatory practice, on both sides of the fence. I am on the recognizable track—I am an old Europeanist teacher, after all—of complicity for the purpose of robust affirmative sabotage.

If we turn again towards Hegel's syntagmatic practice in this crucial paragraph, we discover that the epistemograph moves from certainty to certainty, from *Gewissheit* to *Wahrheit* (Truth), into *Bewusstsein* (consciousness), from mere states to being, from -*heit* to -*sein* words. To get into the syntagmata of gendering, we have to go a completely different route because gender is an instrument of abstractability that is so old that to follow in its tracks is to develop ways of critical intimacy rather different from rational critique. It works before reason, a model which comparative literature has in first-language learning. I am certainly not reading, or even attempting to read, the syntagmata of gendering. To be able to enter that multiply located discursivity, I cannot be the privileged speaker of a lecture. It is something that we always remember and set aside—remembering that it allowed us to set it aside, and so on, indefinitely. Keeping this loosely in mind, I re-enter Hegel's pages.

Let us, then, return to the comparison between Hegel's story and this nested invocation of the inception of feminism in the industrial revolution. *Bewusstsein* at this stage is only a moment on the epistemograph, not what we would colloquially understand by the word 'consciousness'. It contains within itself the possibility of an object, which at this stage is a self-consciousness *as an object*, which also does not, then, resemble what we would colloquially recognize as such. (And the power of the word in the language fights this, of course. That is, here, the double bind of philosophizing like the enemy, not just the fight in the streets, which wants to polarize, self-vanguardize, create a dictatorship of the subaltern, wanting alternativity rather than opposition.) In fact, and of course, the epistemograph is not only about time but it is also a spatial intuition which represents time. Thus, this is not about 'real' self-consciousness. Its only function—the next

step in Hegel's text—is to be able to posit otherness and difference by bringing it to zero. That is what Hegel's text says
in the paragraphs before master–slave begins. The Subject at
this stage cannot 'do' anything. It just nullifies everything by
the programme of Absolute Knowledge, so that something
else can happen. In the philosophical aspect, a principle (with
all the attendant double binds I indicate above) must become
a nothing. If you make it into a narrative, the character has
to act in a certain way, and Hegel hovers in the margins of
that dangerous supplement that would nullify philosophy.

As feminists we must, at this point in the transition from
feudalism to capitalism, with the staging of the emergence
of consciousness, psychologize—play with gender as Hegel
plays with himself. Just as Fanon tells us how to read before
he enters Hegel, so here I try to see how the transgressive
movement in the narrateme in Hegel tells me how to make
the mistake about the narrative of gender, rather than merely
the transition into capitalism as the bearer of reason. Watch
me: if in Hegel the function of *Bewusstsein* is to be able to
posit otherness and difference by bringing itself to zero; this
paradoxical move can be compared—however mistakenly—
to the initial movements of the gender struggle, bringing otherness and difference to zero. For Hegel, when this happens,
the species is separated out from the general flow.

In Marx's *Economic and Philosophical Manuscripts of
1844*, the difference between species-being and species-life
(*Gattungswesen* and *Gattungsleben*) is our Hegelian moment
and as you read Hegel's section, you will see Hegel speaking

of a complete destruction (negation) in order for the emergence of reason; whereas, if you psychologize it, the destruction becomes a recognition. These are not real recognitions or real destructions, but a separating out from the flow of philosophy, the epistemograph as it moves and the species as it traces a merely empirical history. Hegel's philosophy engages in that dangerous auto-eroticism, its own false sublation (*Aufhebung*) into history. The dangerous path of engaging with the auto-eroticism of vanguardism (denied) if you want legitimate entry into the most elite corner of the academy—remaining precariously outside, in the teaching machine.

I am repeating, then, that a certain kind of surreptitious separation also takes place in Hegel as he hints at the narrative of the emergence of capitalism. Of course, this narrative itself is screwed up if you put colonization in. I cannot touch that story here, because we are talking feminism.

When the species is separated out from the general flow, the general flow remains unnamed by Hegel, but, by textual implication, the flow is something that may, unphilosophically, be called life.

How do we know this might be life? The entire passage is written under the sign (two paragraphs above), *An dem Leben*. It is translated into English as 'In the sphere of Life'.[28] But this *an dem* is colloquial German—in life, in terms of life, and the like. This is Hegel's signal to us. He follows the absolutely intractable philosophical argument where there is

28 G. W. F. Hegel, *Phenomenology of Spirit* (A. V. Miller trans.) (Oxford: Oxford University Press, 1977), p. 110.

no human example. On the other hand, the reader might want to read it *an dem Leben*. The Latin expression *sub specie aeternitatis*—in the species of eternity—requests us to remove ourselves from merely empirical considerations. I gave a riff on this when I was talking about the planet in 1997, saying, 'The planet is in the species of alterity'[29] rather than eternity. Hegel is hinting that all of this can also be read under the species of life, as it were—and the storyline comes in as an intended mistake, undoing the philosophical.

On a higher level of abstraction, then, within our mistaken transliteration of philosophy into narrative, we can call this the separating out of gender in a self-conscious mode of abstraction, because the unselfconscious use of gender as instrument of abstraction begins at the inception of the transaction between the sacred and the profane, the establishment of human nature as distinguished from nature as such (ontogeny playing with phylogeny?).

What I have extracted here from Hegel is from the section immediately antecedent to 'Lordship and Bondage'. If we remain within the narrative moment, Hegel encourages us to think that this is a transition from feudalism, since lord and serf are feudal. As I have already mentioned, the word *Herr*, or lord, also means God; and the title of the section might therefore also refer to the sublation of religion, specifically Christianity, into philosophy that also happens in this section and is the burden of both Kant and Hegel. The inauguration

29 Gayatri Chakravorty Spivak, 'Planetarity' in *Death of a Discipline* (New York: Columbia University Press, 2003), pp. 71–102; here, p. 72.

of the merely Christian secularism, its affirmative sabotage by these philosophers into a supposedly unmarked (European) secularism, which is part of our feminist struggle from within Islamophobia, a certain vanguardist feminism which sometimes forgets the lesson I am sketching.

However, for our purposes, it should also be said that the entire historical narrative of gender, women and LGBTQ, can also be read according to the master–slave dialectic, the slave determining the master's mastership. That story is not yet at an end.

I just want to put this as a postscript to reading Fanon reading Hegel, because Fanon is part of the problem here. When we read the text of Fanon, we have to say to ourselves: That story is not yet at an end. I remain uninterested in female leadership, although the glass ceiling of the gender struggle is not unimportant. Here we are looking at the abstract as such emerging as feudalism transitions into capitalism. As the abstract as such emerges, our oldest instrument of abstraction, which is gender, also brings its abstractability and abstracts, according to the laws of capital, its beginning in the nascent capitalism at the end of the European eighteenth century.[30] This is a very complicated story. I will say goodbye to it now. We collectively set aside this story, the reading of the text of Hegel, and the reading of the text of Fanon reading Hegel. We have assembled signals for our future readings of this assemblage of discontinuous

---

30 This postscript comes from Gayatri Chakravorty Spivak, 'Getting a Grip on Gender' (lecture, Atelier Genre Condorcet, Paris, 10 July 2013).

textualities. The adventure is yours. I have carefully shared with you how Fanon prepares me to read Hegel. I say to you: I hope I have made you feel that next time you read an extract, it is necessary to look at the way in which it is being prepared for reading, whether the teacher requires it or not. What the teacher requires is the absolute minimum. Do not let the teacher be your master. And, of course, try to find a way of accessing problems in translation.

QUESTIONS

1. Physical Movement in Territory

When one comments on Kant's lack of travel, one must remember that not everyone is Kant. We cannot take him as an example of the general mind that we are educating, if there is such a thing. On the other hand, travel, or digital travel, does not teach anything by itself. I am more interested in producing people who can use the digital in ways other than you see it being used in places where education is bad: pornography, hacking, stealing, gambling, blogging with absolutely no mind left to think with, crowding as democracy and so on—this is a hopeless situation.

In terms of physical movement, it depends on how you move. How you keep yourself open to the difficult path of critical intimacy, what are your expectations, what are your institutional connections, what is your unexamined cultural-ism for yourself or the other and so on. All of this happens to you from prior preparation—perhaps in literary reading—and not through 'relating to thinking'.

I am trying to (trying to, failing) teach people how to play in the very strong sense, rather than how to produce descriptions. When you teach people how to play, it is the difference between a description of the internal combustion engine and learning to drive. To be able to describe the internal combustion engine is a fantastic thing. On the other hand, to make it a requirement for anybody who learns how to drive is really to bring people with half a mind into a situation where they can lord it over those who can really drive, because they can describe the internal combustion engine!

That is the kind of situation we want to avoid. You see this very much in the medical profession, for example. The best doctors—I am a doctor's daughter and a doctor's granddaughter and a doctor's sister—are against medication. My brother, who was a named cancer surgeon, was derided by his profession, because as oncology improved, he went more and more against surgery. He was no longer interested in slashing and burning. People would ask, 'What kind of a surgeon are you that you are going so much towards oncology?' I come from a stock where such an idea has retained its importance: that playing and finally learning how to play to lose in order to teach is much more important than learning the description of the internal combustion engine.

As to how I relate to thinking—it's the way I relate to living. How? By being alive, I suppose.

2. Recognizing the Universalizable: Žižek and Spinoza

I had thought the question was about some philosopher whose name I had not heard. Now that I can understand, I can say that we do not know about every school of philosophy in India. In order to be able to say something about Cārvāka, don't just say, 'I understand the Cārvāka-ist kings.' Who are they? We are English teachers. If we want to use something from Sanskrit, we should show what statement I am dealing with there. (The only statement of Cārvāka I know is: *Rinam kritva ghritam pivet*—borrow money to drink ghee. It would probably impress foreigners if I quoted it, but it is a meaningless gesture.)

What is behind Žižek is simplified Spinoza, not Cārvāka. The idea that if you happen to see something and it is not part of the universal, you can then try to tease out what is universalizable; but never universalize, because then the element is not there any more. This is a very common-sense solution of the problem of singularity and the ethical universal in Spinoza, which is still useful. We should not, however, as do Hardt and Negri, take it in an unmediated fashion to digital idealism, because Spinoza is writing within an absolutist state. In those united kingdoms where he is writing, there is not even a single currency. He is imagining a good state, an absolutist state, where he thinks this is the way in which the problem will be solved. What is important about his thinking is that it has travelled beyond the historical outlines of its own production. It retains its value for people without any education who have no access to the universal and yet may produce the universilizable, cut off like Nietzsche's *fortgesetzte Zeichenkette*, a continuous sign-chain.[31]

---

31 Friedrich Nietzsche, *On the Genealogy of Morals* (Walter Kaufmann and R. J. Hollingdale trans) (New York: Random House, 1969).

REREADING SPIVAK

I. 'THREE WOMEN'S TEXTS AND A CRITIQUE OF IMPERIALISM'

Let us remember my text from the early 80s by also remembering that Mary Shelley and Jean Rhys are 'white'. This is also what we learnt from Frantz Fanon. Our task is not about uncovering that white people are nasty to brown people, or black people. It is about different ways of relating to others. We must remember that my text recommends Shelley, as it does Rhys, the white Creole (like J. M. Coetzee), as she undoes Jane Eyre. I have never taken any stand against white anything. Such essentializations are always made in bad faith. I taught a class in 1978 where these readings happened. Edward Said and I were no doubt moved by the same waves of social awareness, but I had not yet read *Orientalism* (1978). I was not really thinking about being 'postcolonial'. As soon as I was made aware of that, I became a critic of postcolonialism. I find it difficult to think of Mahasweta Devi as 'indigenous',

In the class, Spivak's remarks were preceded by presentations by Govind Pandit Rathod, MPhil student, and Snober Sataravala, PhD student, both at the Department of English, University of Pune. These papers are available upon request.

because this adjective is now applied to anyone resident out-side of the Euro-US. She is an indefatigable interventionist journalist, an admirable Brahmin troublemaker, ultimately as influenced by history as anybody else, and therefore benevolently feudal. Her 'Pterodactyl'[1] is, I think, a classic. Yet, I think there is a problem in her self-representation as a saviour of the indigenous. We must practice postcoloniality with care and caution.

I had read *Jane Eyre* many times in school. This reading had never occurred to me. What I was going through was a typical autobiographical moment for the conscientious metropolitan educational immigrant in the United States: a feeling comparable to Fanon's sublime discomfort. The demand itself was produced by the American Creed. Anyone in India who has servants does exactly what Jane Eyre does to Bertha. It is completely unrealistic to think that this one novel can convert us in India beyond class. In my text, I suggest that we cannot call Charlotte Brontë a racist. In this country, where the majority religion celebrates as its High Holiday the symbolic killing of a dark-coloured autochthonous buffalo monster, how can we say that there is something wrong with *Jane Eyre*? This is our 'tradition'. We must put this in context with our approach to the writer of the essay, that she, my stereotype of myself, came into this through the United States, whose own philosophy of

1 Mahasweta Devi, 'Pterodactyl, Puran Sahay, and Pirtha' in *Imaginary Maps* (Gayatri Chakravorty Spivak trans.) (New York: Routledge, 1995), pp. 95–196.

classlessness and colour-blindness is, more perceptibly for the immigrant student, compromised. The story of imperialism spoken from Bengal is also a story of the collaboration of the bhadralok class. I have told that story in 'To Construct a Personal Past: Pages from a Memoir', where the real problem I point at is that in Bengal, whether you are right, left or centre, top or bottom or any place, the real goal is bhadraloki.[2] I said this with conviction because it was possible for me to make the case before an audience of Bengalis in Calcutta, in the belly of the beast, not abroad. The scenario of 'Three Women's Texts'[3] is completely different.

What we should really think about when we read a piece like this is that I am an example of Fanon's warning against the immigrant who is loved by the whites. At least I had the good sense to say that when we analyse the story, we should think about the fact that if even such an imagination as Brontë's could be such a victim of such cultural self-representation, how must we be victims of our own? This is a warning against the competitive nationalism from which India is suffering greatly as it 'rises'. The lesson of Brontë's novel is a warning for us, not a diagnosis against white women. Having lived in the United Sates for 52 years, and taught for 48, I ask myself how much does it take to become

2 Gayatri Chakravorty Spivak, 'To Construct a Personal Past: Pages from a Memoir' (Dilip Kumar Roy Memorial Lecture, Sri Aurobindo Institute of Culture, Calcutta, 9 July 2010).

3 Gayatri Chakravorty Spivak, 'Three Women's Texts and a Critique of Imperialism', *Critical Inquiry* 12(1) (Autumn 1985): 243–61.

a Western feminist? Whatever criticism comes from within Western criticism is very different from pointing a finger, especially if we consider the class access which gives permission to do so.

My teachers were what now would be called Dalit Christians. I went to St John's Diocesan Girls' High School. Charubala Dass was my extraordinary principal. Whatever the sins of European colonialism in India, they did at least produce these extraordinary Christians. We must understand my fulminations about 'making the heathen human' in 'Three Women'[4] as also based in a forgetfulness of this epistemological debt, produced by the strong influence of the United States. Here I differ from my brilliant colleague Gauri Viswanathan. I do not believe British education was only a 'mask of conquest'.[5]

It is also a history of class collaboration. I am myself an inheritor of the tradition established in the English Department in Presidency College, Calcutta, by such intellectuals as Henry Vivian Derozio and Michael Madhusudan Dutt, not to mention Bankim Chandra Chattopadhyay. I consider the fact that this is my most anthologized text ('Can the Subaltern Speak?' is merely my most translated text) to be dependent upon a failure to recall the lessons that I have here laid out, particularly important in the Indian context. This is so, I think, because it is an easy text: they are wrong, we are right,

4 Ibid., p. 248.

5 Gauri Viswanathan, *Masks of Conquest: Literary Study and British Rule in India* (New York: Columbia University Press, 1989).

and (although I was careful enough to say I did not think so) Charlotte Brontë was a racist. Think again how much we ourselves must be affected by our construction through our tremendously competitive nationalism; as much and more than Brontë was by the cultural self-representation of Britain in the nineteenth century. This essay is still in print; you have to read it, and I cannot pass on these warnings to the readership except through occasions such as this one, because you chose it—I certainly do not teach this any more.

We must be clear about the sense of 'being borderless' in the study of English literature. Indian writing in English today assumes an 'India' in a way that no regional literature can. However, the borderlessness of English India is available not only to those who produce so-called creative writing in English but also to those who study English literature, teach English literature, and write critical prose in English for all-India distribution. Here we try to be critical of the implicit class-production and use it affirmatively to build a matrix for the study of regional languages as deeply as comparative literature requires. Huge mindset changes are required for this to happen—it is not an easy task. It must, however, be undertaken because only the habit of literary reading will train our unconditional ethical reflexes towards the text of the other.

I wrote 'unlearn your privilege' before I set foot in the activist sphere. You must use your privilege—here class-productive in the literary—and turn it round against itself. Indeed, you cannot unlearn your privilege, and if you keep too focused on trying, you are engaged in a kind of narcissism.

If using your privilege is feudal, within a feudality without feudalism, history has left us no other choice. Proceed with caution, develop some rage against a history that does not allow you a choice. (Incidentally, that is what I would say to the breast-beating, self-described 'bourgeois white males' in my classes in the 1970s and 80s.)

Here, Mahasweta is admirable—she uses her privilege, however feudal. She puts the fear of God into bad police people and bad government officers. This is to engage with the postcolonial nation, rather than imitate a postcolonial theory that simply faults European colonialism. That theory belongs to a history and a place, even symptomatic of a certain moment in the United States. It was incapable of coming to terms with the completely available internationalist and forward-looking postcolonialism of pan-Africanism, which only lacked, like everything else, a viable gender component.

Here, Mahasweta's Mary Oraon is helpful.[6] Mary is a hybrid. Her father is Australian white, and she is a Christian. Mary is not mocked for her lack of prowess in hunting. This is a hunt festival; so neither the women nor the men are really hunting. What Mary does is turn ritual into a 'real' thing. Both Mahasweta and Brontë use the same topos of transforming the other into an animal before they are able to destroy them—a certain kind of humanism, if you like. Bertha in *Jane Eyre* is like a dog, and Tahsildar is turned into an A-N-I-M-A-L. He is not killed because he is a rapist. The

---

6 Mahasweta Devi, 'The Hunt' in *Imaginary Maps* (Gayatri Chakravorty Spivak trans.) (New York: Routledge, 1995), pp. 1–18.

rape is part of the ritual. Mary transforms the act of male sexuality into her weapon. She 'becomes the man', as it were. After the killing, she embraces Budhni and kisses her, and she kills by taking the machete and lifts it up and down, up and down, up and down in a very obvious imitation of male-female sexual intercourse.[7] She negotiates phallocentrism so that it becomes her weapon. This is an interesting idea: Mary is not the authentic tribal but an underclass postcolonial who acts through the impact of colonialism on her.

In 'Breast Giver',[8] caste and class interact. To move with this social textuality is not the kind of postcolonial criticism that faults colonialism, taking literature as evidence. It is in the spirit of such writing that I say, use your class privilege, which allows you to study English literature. You will be amazed by the number of political activists round the world who come from English literary studies. Our polity is hostile to this for the wrong reasons. What is in demand is business and computer science. Don't use your training in English simply to access these fields alone; use this skill to go towards a comparative literature of Indian literatures. Consider our good fortune that we have so many languages, rather than one centralized language that we celebrate. You can absolutely utilize the excellence of English studies: make it your own, sabotage it, turn it round. When you begin to teach, start from your mother tongue, situate it in English

---

7 Ibid., pp. 16–17.

8 Mahasweta Devi, 'Breast Giver' in *Breast Stories* (Gayatri Chakravorty Spivak trans.) (Calcutta: Seagull Books, 1997), pp. 39–76.

and go to another regional language—do not resist Hindi. Remember, it is bad faith to ask, 'How can we do it, because that literature is Western?' The West has a lot of literatures. You do not know any of them but English—a powerful literature, which by now 'belongs' also to India. We must also not think that the West and the subaltern are in a binary opposition. In spite of Edward Said's implicit remark, Gandhi and Nehru were not subalterns.[9] In fact, they were both using varieties of Orientalism in order to think of themselves as 'Indian'.

I put Mahasweta's stories over and against this kind of liberatory Orientalism. If I knew enough about Bengali literature, I would undoubtedly find others as well. Certainly Farhad Mazhar's poetry belongs there. Mahasweta's 'Pterodactyl' is an exquisite story. She makes it very clear in a postscript that just as Mary is not an 'authentic' tribal, so the pterodactyl is obviously not 'real', and whatever happens there is not any anthropologically 'authentic' custom that she had found among the Nagesias. Nothing happens in the text. Puran is shown to be unable to answer a question. It is this inability that allows him to enter the presence of the pterodactyl. He is weeping;

---

9 Edward Said writes in his 1995 Afterword to *Orientalism* (London: Penguin, 2003[1978]): 'I will not deny that I *was* aware, when writing the book, of the subjective truth insinuated by Marx in the little sentence I quoted as one of the book's epigraphs ("They cannot represent themselves; they must be represented"), which is that if you feel you have been denied the chance to speak your piece, you will try extremely hard to get that chance. For indeed, the subaltern *can* speak, as the history of liberation movements in the twentieth century eloquently attests' (p. 335).

he is unable to answer the question. When he enters, the authorial voice begins to speak. This is Mahasweta's version of Orientalism: aborginals, Indo-Europeans, colonialism. But it works for the fiction.

In the early 1980s, practising my own kind of Orientalism, I talked about worlding a world at the beginning of 'Three Women's Texts'. I was referring to Heidegger. In the 80s, looking at the 'The Origin of the Work of Art' (1950), I was too quick to think that Heidegger's idea was of a worlding specifically upon uninscribed earth, since I was moving with my own Orientalism. In fact, in Heidegger, the point is what in common language we would call 'development'. The work worlds and fulfils the earth's destiny, and the earth fights back. 'In setting up a world, the work sets forth the earth [. . .] *The work lets the earth be an earth.*'[10] This has nothing to do with colonialism. I was not reading well. The allegory of the work of art in Heidegger now lets me move from colonialism to globality, to the anthropocene. For the primitive in Heidegger lacks the bestowing grounding leap and head start and is always futureless. In this confidence, he goes on to describe art containing its historical nature as foundation in the history of Western Europe.[11] This simple Euro-teleology, even if legitimized by the many bilateral reversals into alternative epistemologies, still runs the world. This is not just

10 Martin Heidegger, 'The Origin of the Work of Art' in *Poetry, Language, Thought* (Albert Hofstadter trans.) (New York: HarperCollins, 1971), pp. 15–86; here, p. 45.

11 Ibid., p. 74.

colonialism as such. In *What Is Called Thinking*, seminars given in 1951–52, Heidegger suggests that the naming by Western European man of the Being of beings as thinking (or 'thanc'—'thought, thanks, memory [. . .] in the realm of the unspoken', or *enos emmenai*, as in *Parmenides*) is called for by the very nature of the Being of beings.[12] There is nothing to support this claim of Heidegger. It comes out of a major effort of self-worlding, undertaken by European intellectuals anxious to de-Ottomanize, so that Greece could be at the origin of Europe.

Our new task of worlding—we have to make a world, rather than just complain about colonialism—is to instrumentalize the insights, setting them free of the 'as if' world that they had taken as felicitous. In this spirit, a cosmopolitan worlding may think of all worlding as the coming into light concealed from us as unconcealment, as Heidegger says. We must transform Heidegger reading Heraclitus, where he speaks in this way, not as a European reading the Greeks but as a philosopher by chance alighting upon the universilizable.

QUESTIONS

1. Theorizing as Practice

I believe one must prepare oneself to be able to read theory. When I wrote the introduction to *Of Grammatology*, I had never had a course on philosophy either as an undergraduate

12 Martin Heidegger, *What Is Called Thinking* (Fred D. Wieck and J. Glenn Gray trans) (New York: Harper and Row, 1968), p. 153. See also: Spivak, 'Reading *De la grammatologie*'.

or graduate. I was teaching at a very benign university, an enlightened state school, and they gave me a year off. I put myself to school so that I could introduce this book that I had just translated. I learn Chinese and Japanese at such an advanced age for the same kind of reason. I feel that in our time, in the so-called Asian century, someone who works on cultural politics should be able to enter these lingual memories. We do not bulldoze over the linguistic practice of the theorist's work, making argumentative gist. When we are reading the theory, we read it as a primary text, not as something that we are going to apply, not instrumentalizing it, but for its own sake. It becomes part of our mental furniture.

That argument applies even to Marx. In my class, where we have the leisure to read, we read *Capital* as if it were a new thing that had just come across our desk, read it as if we were writing it. It is a very difficult thing, reading theory well. When we are reading this way, we are internalizing. Theorizing is a practice. Our own way of thinking changes, so that when we are reading, all of the theoretical reading begins to organize our reading, not because we are applying it.

Research theory is like athletics. First-class athletes do not think about moves they make. They do not 'apply' what they have been taught. It comes in as a reflex, and if you look at the 'instant replay', you watch muscle memory perform. That is how one 'uses' other people's theory—with respect, preparing oneself to be able to read it, following through. In order to prepare yourself that way, you enter the protocol of the other person's theory, enter its private grammar, so that the theory transforms you.

2. Heidegger

The question of Heidegger has been ably dealt with in Derrida's *Of Spirit* (1989). It is hard to read. You will need to have read Derrida in the intimate way of reading theory that I have just described. Derrida looks at the trajectory of the word *Geist* in Heidegger and how it closes off Heidegger's earlier openness with the *Zusage*—the openness of the question. Derrida shows how Heidegger becomes a Christian humanist and, on the very last page of the book, gives us a picture of racial discrimination coming up like mushrooms in the mulchy soil of the forests of Europe. The book is called *Of Spirit: Heidegger and the Question*. Heidegger gave up the openness of the question, and provided an answer.

3. Aesthetic Education

When I say aesthetic education, I am trying to sabotage Schiller affirmatively. Schiller wrote a collection of letters to the Duke of Württemberg, called *Letters on the Aesthetic Education of Man* (1794). My definition does not come from the German eighteenth century. I am not applying Schiller. I think definitions are halfway houses. I am making a mistake with Schiller, so that my position is not completely critical either. It is also affirmative. I am learning also from the mistake that Schiller made in the era of nascent capitalism. My teacher de Man said that Schiller misunderstood Kant's critique, which was so powerful that it put philosophizing itself into jeopardy. Schiller turned that whole thing into a chiasmus —a balance. My stereotype of myself is not applying de Man. I say I will replace the chiasmus with the double bind:

contradictory instructions coming at the same time. Gregory Bateson thought about this through his study of childhood schizophrenia. Bateson kept working at it, and he finally felt that this was also a description of the most intelligent folks who could actually see this double bind as the nature of life itself.[13] The very act of living—living and dying at the same time—is a double bind.

On the other hand, you must make decisions. There is no not deciding. When you decide, you must mistake the double as two single binds and choose between them. In this choice, the best grounding error is reason. Going through reason is the best way to misunderstand the double bind so that you can make a decision. It is in this sense that I say that aesthetic education is a training of the imagination for this sort of epistemological performance. All human beings are capable of producing simple evidentiary syllogisms. As to what permissible narrative is made to inhabit the syllogism is a relief map. Thunder is God; it has just thundered; God has therefore spoken. The fact that women bear children has led to all kind of obnoxious evidentiary syllogisms. It is in undoing these evidentiary syllogisms that reason as such can be the grounding error.

An epistemological performance is how you construct yourself, or anything, as an object of knowledge. I have been consistently asking you to rethink literature as an object of

13 Gregory Bateson, 'Toward a Theory of Schizophrenia' in *Steps to an Ecology of Mind* (New York: Ballentine Books, 1972), pp. 201–27; 'Double Bind, 1969' in *Steps to an Ecology of Mind* (New York: Ballentine Books, 1972), pp. 271–8.

knowledge, as an instrument of imaginative activism. In *Capital, Volume 1* (1867), for example, Marx was asking the worker to rethink him/herself, not as a victim of capitalism but as an 'agent of production'. That is training the imagination in epistemological performance. This is why Gramsci calls Marx's project 'epistemological'. It is not only epistemological, of course. Epistemological performance is something without which nothing will happen. That does not mean you stop there. Yet, without a training for this kind of shift, nothing survives.

II. 'RIGHTING WRONGS'[14]

1. Coercion and Violence

There is always coercion in education. When I say '*uncoercive rearrangement of desires*',[15] 'uncoercive' does not refer to some sort of willing suspension of coercion. It signals the future anterior: whatever you do, even if it looks like your plan succeeded completely, in the end, something (else) will have happened. Think of Marx's lesson in *The Eighteenth Brumaire* (1854), that the French Revolution resulted in an increase in the power of the executive. We could say that the Bolshevik revolution and the Maoist revolution, by dissolving imperial hierarchies, made it possible for global capitalism to come forth in the absence of the development of the ethical.

14 This section contains responses to questions asked on my essay 'Righting Wrongs', *South Atlantic Quarterly* 103(2–3) (Spring–Summer 2004): 523–81.

15 Ibid., p. 526.

Whatever people plan, something will have happened. Even if it looks like exactly what you wanted has happened, something (else) will have happened. If you know that this is what your planning is worth, then a species of non-coercion comes in, not because you are being nice and non-coercive but because, on psychological ground, there can be no education if there is no shoving and pushing.

Let us then say that the element of non-coercion comes in because the future is undecidable. I am sure historians are familiar with what I am going to describe now, but it made a mark on me—since I am a modernist. On the base of Raja Raja Chola's Brihadishwara Temple in Thanjavur are secular inscriptions in ancient Tamil about marriages, land grants and the like. Here was this great king (early eleventh century) and this exquisite temple with inscriptions written on stone in order to record human history in the house of God. No one can read it, no one knows it, no one thinks about history. There, I understood the meaning of future anteriority. On the other hand, you enter the temple, and you reproduce the existential temporality of the sacred—classroom space.

Who could have asked Raja Raja Chola to be uncoercive? He was an absolutist, benevolent king. History took care of it. He could not coerce the future to work according to his plans. When you think about this, the element of non-coercion is not just some kind of individualistic character trait. The element of non-coercion is a theoretical moment in the task of the teacher.

The changed pedagogy of the humanities—uncoercive rearrangement of desires—can perhaps come to grips with violence as the inevitable weapon of subalternity brought into crisis. I cannot justify violence in any way. But I can try to 'read' violence, enter its protocols. I have tried to 'read' the most terrible violence: suicide bombing.[16] I tried to understand violence against the self in 'Can the Subaltern Speak?' (1988). One understands violence in the Israel–Palestine situation: it will not allow us to be ethical. This is not a justification of violence. The coercion in education or desire in gendered violence are altogether different. When there is no possibility of being heard because no one responds to you and, therefore, violence is taken as a way, you do not think of that violence as a justified means of reparation against the violence done to you. The most one can think of it is: 'I was not allowed to be ethical, my group was not allowed to be ethical; therefore, I am against state-legitimized violence and I will continue to be so.'

I say, therefore, that Fanon does not advocate violence as a means for change. He asks for an understanding of violence, and the understanding that all human lives weigh the same. Today we are talking about injustice in a postcolonial new nation. We cannot read Fanon and decide that he is talking about our present. Even Marx is not writing about our present.

This is where it is important to change the nature of education so that citizenship can come into being. Before he enters Hegel, Fanon talks about the first 20 years of

16 Gayatri Chakravorty Spivak, 'Terror: A Speech after 9/11' in *An Aesthetic Education in the Era of Globalization* (Cambridge, MA: Harvard University Press, 2012), pp. 372–98.

schooling. The kind of violence that is used *in extremis* is not a substitute for being educated, which is all about teacher and student being in a structure of inter-responding.

2. The Vanguard

There is nothing wrong with the vanguard. There is something wrong with the vanguardist attitude. The vanguard can, in fact, be part of democratic representation. Today, in the era of digital globalization, participatory democracy is a pipe dream of the activist middle class, especially when the international civil society is global. In such a situation, representative or parliamentary democracy can make use of the periodically replaced good vanguard. Suppose we forget the actual word 'vanguard'. In fact, in any large group, there is a small group of people who actually get everything done. Sometimes, there are even just one or two persons who actually get everything done. That is the vanguard. If you call it the vanguard, you begin to give it that moral weight, that can make it move towards vanguardism. This is true of all populist movements. It is true of the huge Declarations that you read through the UN—written by the vanguard, alas. Recognition that some people get all the work done is practical, but the statement that what is produced is produced by everyone is simply a lie. You can give the vanguard a committee-type name—'the steering committee'—and for heaven's sake, make it rotate. Otherwise, the government gives the name *swanirbhar dal*—self-reliant groups, hurray!—and the people supposedly in these groups do not know what the name means. Trinamool (grass-roots) Congress is called TMC across the board by the half-educated, uneducated, illiterate subalterns. The grass roots do not know that *trinamool* means grass roots. We should look out for self-declared grass-roots-ism, they-are-doing-it-themselves-ism. There is something good in persistently supplementing vanguardism, so that committed members of the vanguard protect themselves from vanguardism and realize that, in a very real sense, servants are the real vanguard.

3. Producing Resistance

Aniket Jaaware has just remarked that when Shakespeare wrote his works, he did not know that we Indian students of English literature would exist and that, therefore, we should not think about our experience as the context for everything. This, of course, has been my theme. This is the desire which we need to rearrange first as we are getting educated. Paradoxically, this is a practice that strengthens our sense of ourselves. Otherwise we remain so confined within our own justified self-interest, producing more and more justifications and accusing other people, that we begin to think that violence is the only way of solving problems.

4. Unsolicited Comment

'Righting Wrongs' was written sitting on the floor by the light of a hurricane lantern, but my information in there is incorrect. I had not yet properly started in the district of Birbhum in my home state of West Bengal. When I was working only in the district of Purulia, I thought that the situation there was representative. I felt that I could do invisible mending in that context. That was a mistake. Purulia was a special case of romanticization of the tribal. The border area of Birbhum and Jharkhand, where I have worked for the last 15 years, represents the SC/STs in modern India, with no benevolent feudal infantilizing protectionism. They are damaged but modern and feisty.

In Purulia, the leader, a conscientized ex-zamindar (landowner) had no idea, like all benevolent despots, that the real thing was to take his serfs out of their 'tribal identity' and help them be citizens. (That is where Gramsci would come in.) He fought the Communist Party, he fought the police on behalf of his tribal 'subjects', but he had no idea what his own obligation was. He had no idea that the circuit of hegemony, medicine or poison, is where subaltern education should go, rather than the subaltern being preserved like the 'heritages' preserved by the World Monuments Fund.

It is because of this state of preservation that I wrote in 'Righting Wrongs' that the task of the teacher was to learn the fabric of the torn culture so well that she can then do invisible mending.[17] That was based on bad evidence, and it is something that I wanted to share with you before you got your energies together to ask me another question.

5. Before Will

This is the passage by me that was quoted in the question:

> These are only analogies, to be found in an Oxford Amnesty series collection and in Saussure. They

17 Spivak, 'Righting Wrongs', p. 548.

work in the following way: if we can grasp that all human beings are genetically written before will; and if we can grasp that all human children access language that is 'outside', as mother tongue; then, on these structural models, we might grasp the assumption that the human being is human in answer to an 'outside call'. We can grasp the structure of the role of alterity at work in subordinate cultures, by way of these analogies. The word *before* in 'before the will' is here used to mean logical and chronological priority as well as 'in front of'. The difference is historical, not essential. It is because I believe that right/responsibility can be shared by everyone in the persistent mode of 'to come' that I keep insisting on supplemental pedagogy, on both sides.[18]

I would not be able to explain it as well myself if I had not learnt from Derrida's explanation; so the thing to do is to have the Derridean text in front of us in order to be able to see what I learnt.[19] 'Before will' is also a reference to a phrase in Kafka that translates into French as *devant la loi*, 'before the law'—a description of the unbelievable predicament that Joseph K. undergoes in *The Trial* (1925): of not getting inside the gates. He is there every day in front of the door, before the gate, before the law. This is a moment of intertextuality

18 Ibid., p. 545.

19 Jacques Derrida, 'Force of Law: The "Mystical Foundation of Authority"' (Mary Quaintance trans.) in David Gray Carlson, Drucilla Cornell and Michel Rosenfeld (eds), *Deconstruction and the Possibility of Justice* (New York: Routledge, 1992), pp. 3–67.

for those who would recognize the phrase. Whoever among you described the terrible crisis which was not allowing him/her to attach him/herself to uncoercive rearrangement of desire (a reference to an informal discussion not included in our text) would find in Kafka an extraordinary description of how bourgeois civil society can break down. So, rather than describe it as your own terrible predicament, look to see how other texts have done it in ways that travel all over the world, not just confined to the text by Franz Kafka, which already establishes a connection with the extensive Kafka readership.

I am learning to 'be haunted' by Kafka's novel, rather than reading it as evidence or an imitative model, as I am trying to understand the difficulty of myself as an other for my subaltern clientele, myself a gentlewoman from the capital, class and caste enemy from abroad. I am trying to use my learnt expertise at 'reading' as student, literary critic and teacher and, even so, as I told you, I was wrong the first time because I took the benevolent despots' anthropologization as 'reality'. My basic premise was not wrong but the people with whom I worked were preserved tribals, anthropologically preserved by the good will of the bhadralok. My own bogus arithmetical equality—democracy reduced to one vote for each—had not come through as it does in Birbhum. This bottom line of democracy is used for buying and stealing votes, because they are counted—arithmetical. I am worth one, and so is each of them, unless they are cheating. At least the teacher is trying blindly to produce the desire not to cheat, by attempting to access the place before the will, used in learning our shared mother tongue by children and workers, as literary reading does, and trying to make the appropriate ones recognize the big rule of cheating for the serious capitalists: when you lose, you change the rules of the game —'before the law'.

That is the complicity of 'before the will' and 'before the law', which is bigger than just my will. The principle of the will is a huge thing. It relates to the place of the desire in Hegel: the will to power through knowledge, the will to power through gender, through class, through any bit of *l'irréductible vis-à-vis* (Foucault: irreducible face-to-face in the sub-individual available for power inscription,[20] mistranslated in English) available, among the available permissible narratives, for transforming my life into a story that helps me live. The will is a thing that allows uninstructed parents to push their children towards a certain kind of success which then will destroy the world, out of love. In Kafka's novel, this 'before the will' has to do with waiting patiently to have the door opened, which will in fact never open, and the person who is waiting will be killed with a knife like a dog. That is the end of the story, which Coetzee opens up in *Disgrace* (1999). The end of Kafka's novel, not Kafka himself, says the shame will outlast my death. Kafka does not say it; Joseph K. is made to say it. The shame is the absolute failure of the principles of bourgeois civil society (without, the teacher dreams, an

---

20 Michel Foucault, 'Le Dispositif de Sexualité' in *Histoire de la Sexualité I: La Volonté de Savoir* (Paris: Éditions Gallimard, 1976), pp. 107–73; here, p. 127. Translated as 'irreducible opposite' in 'The Deployment of Sexuality' in *The History of Sexuality*, VOL. 1, *The Will to Knowledge* (Robert Hurley trans.) (London: Penguin, 1978), pp. 77–131; here, p. 96.

uncoercive rearrangement of the desire to cheat or to follow rules blindly). What is engaged here, through intertextuality, is that entire argument—Kafka, Foucault, Derrida—as the teacher is trying to engage the law as desire by engaging in children, fellow teachers and herself, the place before the will, where access to language is acquired.

Why am I saying that these are only analogies to be found in an Oxford Amnesty Lectures series and in Saussure? I should have put a footnote there. Because this talk was first given at an Amnesty International benefit at Oxford. Why was I invited to give that talk? I do, of course, support Amnesty International. They are massively helpful in top-down intervention that must bypass the absence of real education due to class apartheid. For example, I have myself been able to intervene through them for the release of Farhad Mazhar from jail when he was imprisoned with no charge, no trial and no access to habeas corpus; and in raising some public awareness of the desire for ethnic power in the polity that would vote— democracy as body count, again—for Aung San Suu Kyi.

So, even as I deeply appreciate the usefulness of Amnesty International, I remain, of course, committed to the long-term change which will make such organizations only marginally necessary as the last resort. I was, therefore, at that period not on call for such organizations. (The situation has changed somewhat since I won the Kyoto Prize in Thought and Ethics in 2012.)

But this was 2001. I was in London because I have to keep on giving lectures to pay for the tickets to travel comfortably three, four, five times a year to arrive rested at the rural schools; otherwise, the centuries and millennia of caste habit of taking care of the tired bhadramahila would take over and I would not be able to work for them there at all. As a result, unfortunately, when I am coming in from the schools, if there is a conference immediately, I have to enter my other world without any debriefing. It is a shock. There was that year a conference called 'Travel and the Nation' in London, which was paying a nice, hefty business-class round trip, contributing to my ticket. I never buy my own ticket. I only go to Birbhum, as I say to my co-workers, *Noukar shubidha pailay*—'if I get the advantage of a boat, a ferry', by way of lecture invites. They all know why my visits are irregular.

I came into this conference and it was the Indian-British glamorizing themselves as sufferers, which was awful by contrast to the subalterns accepting wretchedness as normal. And they were surrounded by benevolent white British persons, who were getting their catharsis by emoting with these people. (Alas, many of them are and would like to be involved with the international civil society groups aided by the local feudals masquerading as 'ethnic' that produce misleading statistics!)

Sitting in that crowd, I was thinking that in Purulia, I was not hearing complaints, except the acute gender-political song: 'When I grow old and die, I will sit on a branch and I will twirl my moustache.' In other words, I want to be a man when I die. Of course they composed this, because, by the law of the oral formulaic, they were composers. I was so irritated by what was happening all round me in London that I began talking about how I had learnt nation-think from the tribals. It was a little benevolent, but nonetheless. I learnt from the women, of course, because it was the women, relatively untouched by the rural middle class, who could still do the oral formulaic—perhaps they cannot any more. The men had lost it because they had more contact, and the oral formulaic is not just enforced illiteracy but 'writing' as access to the great genealogical memories (Derrida, again, correcting Lévi-Strauss on the Nambikwara).[21] I could not keep up with them, but would sing with them.

So I sang some of these songs to demonstrate how the principle of equivalence in oral formulaic composition actually puts the so-called nation-state in a position of equivalence. I wrote about this in 'Nationalism and the Imagination' (2012). So then the benevolent British, the Amnesty people, must have said: 'Wow. This woman is not just the victim of racism living in London. *Hey*. She seems to know something more worth being benevolent about.' Two weeks later, I received an invitation to give an Amnesty International talk. Most of 'Righting Wrongs' was, indeed, written in the village of Jonara, sitting with my legs out, because there was no furniture. I had brought from the Hong Kong University of Science and Technology, which was also contributing a good bit,

21 Jacques Derrida, 'The Violence of the Letter: From Lévi-Strauss to Rousseau' in *Of Grammatology* (Gayatri Chakravorty Spivak trans.) (Baltimore, MD: Johns Hopkins University Press, 1976), pp. 101–40.

checked out by my research assistant there, a wonderful man called Wai-Lim Yip, two suitcases full of books so that I could write the damn thing. The essay is full of footnotes. So get the irony: I was writing all of the things that you could not understand in a place where people had no advantages at all, and I had to be absolutely comprehensible to them because that was my task.

When I finished, I sent Ashish, my local assistant, to the county town of Purulia, which had a post office, to send the books back to Hong Kong by air mail. He came back smiling and said: 'Didi, this is the first time in living memory that air mail has been used by the General Post Office in Purulia town, and all of the workers, especially the postmaster, were telling me that we must keep up the honour of our country— *desher shamman rakhha korte hobe.*' The postage was Rs 600. They did not have stamps of a higher denomination than Rs 10. There were stamps all over the box. If I had wanted to prove to the world that I was a real heroine, I would have included this part of the story in the essay in a pious, journalistic, exploratory mode, explaining how I had gone into the bushes in order to get these insights, et cetera. Of course, I had not gone into the bushes, I was perfectly comfortable, as far as you can be if you have a spinal problem and no furniture—but that can happen anywhere.

I have shared this story with you because this is why I am saying that in an Amnesty International essay, the only analogy that I can give will be from Saussure. I am insisting that the 'Western' theory that I learnt and teach helped me but not enough, because all analogies are false. Indeed, I do not have those pieties any more because I have escaped—was turned out because of, really, another story—the benevolent despotism of the bhadralok.

Let me give you another example of 'before will'. I have had sciatica since I was very young, which has now turned to spinal stenosis. At five months, when the infant Gayatri's back straightened, some 'I' 'read' some genetic inscription wrong, so that the lowest lumbar vertebra is on one side sacral. Instead of being like a nut, it is like a wing-screw. It is fused with the pelvic girdle, so the hole through which the great sciatic nerve passes pinches the nerve. Who read the genetic inscription wrong? I was five months old. It was 'I' but not the intending subject. It changed my life for ever. I got sciatica, but the subject that read the genetic inscription wrong—even using the word 'wrong' there is a problem, because since the genetic inscription was being read by this whole DNA collection in this way, it was right for this body— disease was normality, 'before the will'.

This is a contemporary philosophical turn upon the body-mind problem. Genomics scholars find a restricted ethics built on rational choice boring. They also do not try to give ethical solutions. They find our kind of thinking about an unconditional ethics more interesting because there is so much that is unconditional in the human being as a passage for DNA. At any rate, that is what I was talking about when I said genetically inscribed before will. When it comes to genetic inscription, you cannot, in fact, answer the question: Who wills?

To manage the insight into such things, I turn to the intuition of the transcendental in *adrishto*—radical alterity inscribing life as the unseen. Hegel thinks of that as the stages of the phenomenological epistemograph prior to the kicking in of the master–slave dialectic. In 'Translation as Culture' (2000) and 'Rethinking Comparativism' (2009), digesting Melanie Klein, I have described the access to the mother tongue before will in the following way: the infant invents a language.[22] The parents learn the infant's language. The parents, on the other hand, live within a language that has a history before the parents were born or the infant was born and will continue to have a history after the parents die and the infant dies. In this parent–infant transaction of first-language learning (it can be a first language, it can be first languages—it does not have to be a mother tongue), where they insert the infant's language, in order to be able to work with it, into the named language(s) which they inhabit. They say that the child relates to parts of the parent's body (because that is all that the child is perceiving right then and all the child has got right then) through this language transaction, his/her own invented one. All of this is happening without any theorizing. The child is theorizing— but how does an infant theorize? The language learning is, through these organs/parts of the parents as bits of alphabet, if you like, constructing a kind of ethical sign system, on the basic +/- artificial-intelligence model, but it is actually *exactly not* artificial or totally artificial *as* natural. Before will.

22 See Gayatri Chakravorty Spivak, 'Translation as Culture', *Parallax* 6(1) (2000): 13–24; 'Rethinking Comparativism', *New Literary History* 40(3) (Summer 2009): 609–26.

In that situation of constructing ethical semiosis, the distinctions between need and desire, pleasure and satisfaction, dissatisfaction and withholding—ethical elements—are being engaged before the developed will which stands in social discourse for the self. This is the thing the teacher wants to nurture, without guarantees, wanting to train for epistemological performance. This can happen in any language (and this is what I said in 'Rethinking Comparativism'), because if the infant learns that language as an infant, even if the parents are completely illiterate, stupid, total drunkards, murderers and thieves, this—what I just described —is happening. It is not a matter of parental instruction, which is also important, but secondary. It is a process that happens. Any language, even the most ignored, private language that has never had a grammar—if the infant learns it, this can happen in it. 'Before will' refers to the logical will, because the infant does have a certain kind of will. 'Before' is not just chronological but, as Freud says, 'metapsychological'.[23] The psychology of the infant has not yet developed, and so the circuits that are activated in the infant are metapsychological—an incredible kind of planting.

The idea that it is an outside call and that, therefore, human beings are made human through the call of the other seems to me, now, to be too sentimental. In 'Righting Wrongs',

---

23 Sigmund Freud, 'Beyond the Pleasure Principle' (1920) in *The Standard Edition of the Complete Psychological Works of Sigmund Freud* (James Strachey ed.), VOL. 18, '*Beyond the Pleasure Principle*', '*Group Psychology*', *and Other Works* (James Strachey with Anna Freud, Alix Strachey and Alan Tyson trans) (London: Hogarth, 1955), pp. 7–64.

I could go to the ethical claim that subaltern people have guarded this in their civilization. What can you be but other-worldly if you are constantly looked after by a zamindar? There is no room for the self in this infantilization. There is, in fact, no way that you can have any testing of how the subaltern really operates. None. History is what hurts. I sense it now.

This may be true about all languages because they are learnt and produced by infants. But on another level, you must fight for power resources, especially financial in today's India, or anywhere, for languages that have been politically denied any social presence. This is a different issue from being able to assume that any language—if it is a language—is capable of setting the metapsychological circuits of a human being into motion by the infant's learning of it as the language with which to manipulate the world. This comes before literacy, numeracy, institutional education. That is the situation 'before will'. I am, of course, revising 'Righting Wrongs' in light of new experience. I no longer believe that right and responsibility can be shared by everyone in the per-sistent mode of 'to come'. I now believe that this has to be created epistemologically as a collectivity of minds through the philosophy of education that I cannot yet devise because of the distance, historically established by my caste and class, between my subaltern clientele and me, more compli-cated than pre-Party-formation, than producing collectivities engaged against oppression, not the pedagogy of the oppressed—all good things. I no longer believe that it hap-pens naturally from subaltern cultures, for if it could, histor-ical crimes could be undone rather easily!

In Birbhum, because the subaltern classes have not been preserved in some kind of anthropological subservience, I see how cognitively damaged they are. I am not against rote learning when necessary. I did, in fact, completely memorize my economics and history papers, because for English Honours, I wanted a first class. I told my mother, 'Ma, you read the question papers for the last 20 years and prepare suggestions for me, and remember that I am only going to study one weekend for my economics paper. Bangla, I'll do all right'—and I did come first—'Bangla, I don't have to study, but history and economics, Ma. You make the questions and I'm going to memorize the answers flat that weekend. So do good, because otherwise I'm going to fail.' She was amazing. Deficit financing, all kinds of stuff. I memorized the figures, everything. Do not ask me what they mean—who knows. This proves that I also can use rote if necessary. But was this a good way to learn economics and history? I did not get a star, because she did not get three topics. She missed Richelieu. I could do that, I had read Alexandre Dumas, and I wrote English well. She missed the zamindari system. I could do that, I had read Sarat Chandra, I could write English well. The one that she missed which made me miss the star was the '1936 Soviet Constitution' (amended 1944). This I could not make up, even if I knew English well. I could, therefore, use rote when necessary. What troubles me among the subaltern classes is nothing but rote answers to pre-set incomprehensible questions learnt without comprehension, further damaging the possibility of intellectual labour for cognitive instruments destroyed by millenial oppression.

One of my nieces is an activist, the international cam-
paigner for Pesticide Action Network. At that time, she had
just graduated in architecture from Delhi University and had
enrolled in University College London. I took her to my talk.
When I had given my talk, I asked her what she thought. I
was expecting: 'Really good, really good.' She said: 'Well, you
know, there was no organization to your talk. I have heard
better talks.' And she mentioned a genuinely straight-line-type
social-science intellectual and said: 'That's a good talk.' I was
very disheartened. I said: 'Pshaw!' She told me much later:
'Mashi, I think of that exchange now that I work and I see
what you do. I can't take those words back, can I? But that's
Delhi University. We don't like Calcutta intellectuals, Mashi.
That's all it was; nothing more.' However, in response to her
comment, and a subsequent similar comment by a smart,
young first-year student at Halifax University in Canada, who
certainly knew noting about the Delhi–Calcutta conflict, on
the eve, as it happens, of the Arab Spring, upon which I com-
mented then and there in response to requests by Arab intellectuals, I now try to offer a summary of my argument at the
end of each talk—because I am not, in fact, disorganized—
just *anders determiniert* (Freud)—otherwise determined, a
description of 'overdetermined'. Before will?

WHAT HAPPENS IN THE TEXT?
J. M. Coetzee's *Summertime* and Elizabeth Gaskell's
North and South

Although the two papers were genuinely excellent, they, in the way of good papers, did also present the novel as evidence for a certain kind of theory shuttling between Barthes and Benjamin and Bakhtin—nice 'B' pattern there!—evidence for the ideas of postmodern narrative, metanarrative, self-referential writing and so on. When we read, we try to resist these impulses, and remember that what happens in the novel is prose.

We start, then, with the question: What happens? Not: How does this prove that this is a postmodern text? We ask further: Why is this ruse there? We try to plot out the desire in the novel, of the novel. In terms of Coetzee's 'writerliness', we remember that the novel is held between *Dusklands* (1974) and *Disgrace* (1999). In the first section of *Summertime*,[1] the Julia section, Coetzee the character brings *Dusklands* to Julia, and comments on it. Julia expresses her opinion about

In the class, Spivak's remarks were preceded by presentations by Chetan Sonawane, PhD student, and Namrata Sathe, MPhil student, both at the Department of English, University of Pune. These papers are available upon request.

1 J. M. Coetzee, *Summertime: Scenes from a Provincial Life* (New York: Penguin, 2009), hereafter cited in the text as S with page reference following.

Dusklands, which is clearly an invitation to the reader of *Summertime* to consult *Dusklands*, and to plot a date: 1974. We keep that in mind. The novel is not just about how novels are written. It is an autobiography. There is a 'real' date, that brings the heteronormative back in a ring to the existentially impoverished autonormativity of 'the same date', the date of publication of *Dusklands*, and *Disgrace*. Coetzee constructs a character—Sophie, his colleague—who is made to say that, after *Disgrace*, 'I did not read.'

In other words, there is something in this book that asserts itself as going past the *Dusklands–Disgrace* section of Coetzee's writings. What could it be? Our first clue is that it is written by the Coetzee who leaves South Africa.

It is like a puzzle the reader is being asked to work out. These are 'facts'. We are perhaps even asked to consider the objections brought by the African National Congress to *Disgrace*. And I ask you, then, to read my essay on *Disgrace*, which points out that that is a failure in reading. The 'author factor' is very much there, his name is there, the Nobel Prize is there—the novel is not in a vacuum but, like the cetology pages in *Moby-Dick* (1851), shows us the usefulness and limits of mere fact, in reading, so that we do not reduce the literary to evidence. We remember that the warnings about intentional fallacy—good warnings offered by the New Criticism in the United States—were historically inscribed during the Cold War, an abdication of responsibility. Here the author, instead of being 'outside' the text, is textualized. US-style postmodernism has not been able to accommodate this. But the people who are called (alas, wrongly, ever since Habermas' 1983 interview)[2] the major 'postmoderns' explore the textuality of lives, and Coetzee, in with them, is engaging that interest. Author-as-character.

The author-as-character might have provided us with a little more material to go past the *Dusklands–Disgrace* section of Coetzee's writings. Let us turn to *The Childhood of Jesus*, which appeared in 2013.

Simón and David, a man and a boy, arrive by boat to find a new life. David's father perished in an accident during the trip. David had a letter giving specifics of his mother. This was also lost. It is, then, an undocumented migrant child accompanied by an unrelated adult who arrives at the inn, looking for his mother. The title of the book makes us think this is the child Jesus and we are not wrong. Simón 'finds' David's mother, by intuition, not evidence. After problems with regular schooling because he is a miracle child, Simón and Inés, the 'found' mother, escape the law and are on the road in a car, in search of a new life again.[3]

2 Jürgen Habermas, 'Conservative Politics, Work, Socialism and Utopia Today', interview by Hans-Ulrich Beck, 2 April 1983 (Peter Dews trans.) in Peter Dews (ed.), *Autonomy and Solidarity: Interviews with Jürgen Habermas* (London: Verso, 1991), pp. 131–46. See also Jürgen Habermas, 'Modernity Versus Postmodernity' (Seyla Ben-Habib trans.), *New German Critique* 22 (Winter 1981): 3–14.

3 This is a modified extract from Gayatri Chakravorty Spivak, 'Lie Down in the Karoo: An Antidote to the Anthropocene', review of *The Childhood of Jesus* by J. M. Coetzee, *Public Books*, 1 June 2014. Available at: http://www.-publicbooks.org/fiction/lie-down-in-the-karoo-an-antidote-to-the-anthropoc ene- (last accessed on 8 August 2014).

This is the narrative of *The Childhood of Jesus*. As usual, Coetzee sets up rhetorical signals, teaching us how to 'read' him. We remind ourselves that he has tried to access the mindset of those unlike him by staging their story in novels—derelicts (*The Life and Times of Michael K.*, 1983), 'barbarian' females (*Waiting for the Barbarians*, 1980), old women (*The Age of Iron*, 1990, the Elizabeth Costello novels), the colonized and enslaved (*Foe*, 1986)—the list goes on. And he stages actively and repeatedly the question of the white Creole's right to honesty and love of/in the postcolonial nation, to move beyond mere obedience to the political correctness of nothing but distant admiration of the formerly colonized. This last question has occupied perhaps all of his books, but more pointedly, *Disgrace*, the peculiar 'autobiographical' books *Boyhood* (1997), *Youth* (2002), *Summertime*, and this. I have tried to track him, uncertainly.

In *Boyhood*, manipulating 'facts' as usual, a fictive John Coetzee as a boy, in the third person, thinks of the 'Karoo' where, in Voëlfontein, his family had a farm:

> [H]e loves every stone of it, every bush, every blade
> of grass, loves the birds that give it its name, birds
> that, as dusk falls, gather in their thousands in the
> trees around the fountain, calling to each other,
> murmuring, ruffling their feathers, settling for the
> night. It is not conceivable that another person could
> love the farm as he does. [. . .] Would that be the
> price, if he were to give up going to school and plead
> to live here on the farm: that he would have to stop

asking questions, obey all the *mustn'ts*, just do as he was told? Would he be prepared to knuckle down and pay that price? Is there no way of living in the Karoo—the only place in the world where he wants to be—as he wants to live: without belonging to a family? [. . .] There is not enough time in a single life to know all of Voëlfontein, know its every stone and bush. No time can be enough when one loves a place with such devouring love.[4]

Some years ago, in *Nationalism and the Imagination*, I wrote: This rock-bottom comfort in one's language and one's home with which nationalism conjures is not a positive affect—when there is nothing but this, as I saw with these folks I worked with.[5] I would not have known this as a metropolitan Calcutta person at the time of Independence, at the inception of the new nation-state from an established nationalism. When there is nothing but this, its working is simply a thereness. Please remember that I am not talking about resistance groups but about people who accept wretchedness as normality. That is the subaltern, those are the folks that I worked with. I learnt this from below. When this comfort is taken away, there is a feeling of helplessness, loss of orientation, dependency, but no nation thing.

4 J. M. Coetzee, *Boyhood: Scenes from Provincial Life* (New York: Penguin, 1997), pp. 80, 91.
5 See Gayatri Chakravorty Spivak, *Nationalism and the Imagination* (London: Seagull Books, 2010).

Has the colonizing elite earned the right to access this subaltern helplessness? Is history so much larger than personal affect that only political correctness is allowed?

In *Summertime*, John Coetzee's love of the Karoo is given in a conversation reported by his cousin Margot, to Vincent, the interviewer. Coetzee tells her his secret: "'Don't reveal that to Carol,' he—John, her cousin—says. "Don't tell her, with her satirical tongue, how I feel about the Karoo. If you do, I'll never hear the end of it"' (S: 98).

The passage just above these words corroborates my own sense of the nature of this affect, shared by the human with the top primates. In the reported conversation, Coetzee the cousin is made to cite, for Margot somewhat gratuitously, Eugène Marais's *My Friends the Baboons* (1939):

> 'He writes that at nightfall, when the troop stopped foraging and watched the sun go down, he could detect in the eyes of the older baboons the stirrings of melancholy, the birth of a first awareness of their own mortality.' [. . .] 'I understand what the old male baboon was thinking as he watched the sun go down, the troop leader, the one Marais was closest to. Never again, he was thinking: *Just one life and then never again. Never, never, never.* That is what the Karoo does to me too. It fills me with melancholy. It spoils me for life.' She still does not see what baboons have to do with the Karoo or their childhood years, but she is not going to let on (S: 96–7).

I am sitting in Ghana, reading Du Bois's personal copies of the obvious nineteenth-century texts describing South Africa, the most obvious being George Stow's posthumously published *Native Races of South Africa* (1905), where the vicious extermination policy of the Dutch, and then the Boer farmers—the latter Coetzee's ancestors—are recounted, sometimes by eyewitness colonial participants. 'Coetzee' as a surname is cited both among the colonists and the so-called Bastaards. It makes us ask again, and perhaps Coetzee does, how much larger is history than personal goodwill? Should this question be withheld regarding precolonial violence, depredations, slave trading, et cetera? Nothing of this is in *The Childhood of Jesus.*[6] My reading is contaminated by what seems deep background.[7]

It now the moment to open *Dusklands*, John's reported gift to Julia. The book contains two novellas—first, 'The Vietnam Project', where a textually schizophrenic author uses a narrator, deeply resentful of 'Coetzee', to act out a descent into insanity as what we have learnt to call 'post-traumatic stress

6 The only possible, and highly improbable, connection might be the name of the city where Simón and David are born again—Novilla—as recalling Queen Novili, the granddaughter of the last great Xhosa chief Kreli (John Henderson Soga, *The Ama-Xosa: Life and Customs* [Alice: Lovedale Press, 1932], p. 106); Du Bois's private collction; cited obviously not as 'current research' but 'colonial classics'.

7 I have asked myself this question continually over the last 30 years as I try to train teachers among the rural landless Dalits in my home state. My caste and class have millennially denied them the right to intellectual labour, oppressed them in many cruel material ways and convinced them of their social and spiritual inferiority.

syndrome' after Vietnam. The second novella is 'The Narrative of Jacobus Coetzee', the fictionalized account (comparable in inspiration to Assia Djebar's imagining of women's moments in a mediaeval Arabic text in *Far from Madina*, 1994) of an actual eighteenth-century deposition by an actual ancestor of the author, the account itself also included in the text. Already in this first publication, we see the fictive staging of a 'Coetzee' implicated in imperialism. A certain historical continuity of exterminatory imperialism is established, perhaps. In *Summertime*, we are asked to attend to it. In a curious passage in *Dusklands*, 'Coetzee', commenting on Jacobus Coetzee, establishes a peculiar connection between the United States and South Africa:

> We may in passing pause to glance with sorrow at the pusillanimous policy of the [Dutch East India] Company in regard to White colonization, with regret and puzzlement at the stasis of the Netherlands population during the eighteenth century (sloth? self-satisfaction?), and with wistful admiration at the growth of the United States, which in the same era increased the White population geometrically and checked its native population growth so effectively that by 1870 there were fewer Indians than ever before.[8]

The Childhood of Jesus seems to undo 'The Vietnam Project' (D: 1–50), where the biological father stabs the child to

---

8 J. M. Coetzee, *Dusklands* (New York: Penguin, 1982[1974]), p. 112, hereafter cited in the text as D with page reference following.

hold it from its biological mother. In the fictionalized narrative of Jacobus Coetzee, apart from historical racism combined with admiration and implausible philosophical speculation, most of the account is of the details of a tremendous diarrhoea suffered by the protagonist and his epistemological performance of self-recovery with the passing of 'a healthy stool' (D: 93). If the invocation of the baboon in the 2009 text calls up the animal's attachment to space, the 1974 text recounts the mingling of master and man in an inscription of the soil that cannot be erased. A transformation of Levinas' idea of the human as object as the inauguration of the ethical:[9]

> From the scalp and beard, dead hair and scales. From the ears, crumbs of wax. From the nose, mucus and blood (Klawer, Dikkop [Hottentot followers], a fall and blows respectively). From the eyes, tears and a rheumy paste. From the mouth, blood, rotten teeth, calculus, phlegm, vomit. From the skin, pus, blood, scabs, weeping plasma (Plaatje [Hottentot follower], a gunpowder burn), sweat, sebum, scales, hair. Nail fragments, interdigital decay. Urine and the minuter kidneystones (Cape water is rich in alkalis). Smegma (circumcision is confined to the Bantu). Faecal matter, blood, pus (Dikkop, poison). Semen (all). These relicts, deposited over Southern Africa in two swathes, soon disappeared under sun, wind,

9 Emmanuel Levinas, *Otherwise Than Being, or Beyond Essence* (Alphonso Lingis trans.) (Pittsburgh, PA: Duquesne University Press, 1998).

rain, and the attentions of the insect kingdom, though their atomic constituents are still of course among us. *Scripta manent* (D: 119).

I have cited these texts to consolidate my intuition that *The Childhood of Jesus* is the last in a line of texts writing the attachment to land outside of the topology of colonialism.

I believe the new land of *The Childhood of Jesus*, without history, the place of active forgetfulness (Nietzsche), is the way for a postcolonial white Creole subject to imagine the best of precolonial Africa. Again and again, Simón asks 'Why?' and accedes to belief from reason and irony at last. Simón is his new name—perhaps an allusion to Simon Peter, who accompanied Jesus and saw his transfiguration, as does this Simón in the hospital: 'The chariot is made of ivory or some metal inlaid with ivory, and is drawn by two white horses. [. . .] Grasping the reins in one hand, holding the other hand aloft in a regal gesture, is the boy, naked save for a cotton loincloth.'[10]

Perhaps in such a man's vision, the child Jesus, brought by him to a new life, can grow only in such a society—only for a while, of course—because the fully grown Jesus can only be imagined, in the mode of a counterfactual time out of time, 'to come'. Like James Joyce's Gabriel Conroy, Simón is shown to be able to imagine that which he cannot know.[11]

10 J. M. Coetzee, *The Childhood of Jesus* (New York: Penguin, 2013), pp. 237–8, hereafter cited in the text as CJ with page reference following.
11 See James Joyce, 'The Dead' in *Dubliners* (New York: Viking, 1967[1914]), pp. 175–224.

Most societies are abstractly constructed by perceived sexual difference. This is the easiest material difference that people can perceive. This is the tacit global, before the globe was imagined by men of science. Coetzee stages the entire story within this difference, round the questions of the search for the mother, and the virgin birth. There is a reasonable female, Elena, who argues strongly against Simón's intuitive choice of the mother as *David's* mother, in spite of the fact that she is a 30-year-old virgin—there is an embarrassing episode with a sanitary napkin (CJ: 135)—whom Simón and David have accidentally encountered in a place found by mistake because the map is wrong.[12]

Coetzee's story displays a rarefied (and fascinatingly dull) primitive socialism without locatable geographical lineaments. It is into such a society that everyone comes to be born again. The date of their arrival is their new birthday (CJ: 201). It is a society without irony, without memory, where nobody understands why an activity must be justified in terms of an end rather than simply celebrated as labour, where there is a good deal of useless bureaucracy, and where physical and intellectual appetites are expected to be denied. It is to such a society that the child Jesus must come in order to supersede it and run from reasonable educational principles that cannot

12 Incidentally, accessing by mistake is a mini-topos. In Mahasweta Devi's 'Pterodactyl', the story of an Indian journalist going to investigate a tribal area where a pterodactyl has appeared, for example, it is only when the journalist is unable to answer the question posed by the tribals that he finds himself admitted to the enclosure where the ancient bird is lodged. Examples can be multiplied.

understand his miraculous being. The 'mother' that Simón intuitively recognizes comes from a *Residencia* that seems to belong to the vague outlines of an older order, perhaps even reminiscent of Coetzee's memory of his own mother's life before his parents married, at least as reported by the author-as-character of *Boyhood*.[13]

The languages that are invoked in the novel cannot be named. Everyone is supposedly speaking Spanish, Simón and David badly. Arriving at page 66, we cannot be sure that that is indeed the language which is normally called Spanish for, on page 67, a passage in German is represented as English, presumably to show that the English text is not English. How does it feel, the text might be asking, to inhabit an unknown but translated episteme? What might be staged is the sanctioned ignorance of both the biblical and African languages.

> Would I be able to translate myself soberly across the told tale, getting back to a dull, decent farmer's life in the shortest possible time, or would I weaken and in a fit of boredom set out down a new path, implicate myself in a new life, perhaps the life of the white Bushman that had been hinting itself to me?
> (D: 99)

This had been the earlier question in *Dusklands*. When, at a certain point, languages are listed in *The Childhood of Jesus*—this is the list: 'Portuguese . . . Catalan . . . Galician . . . Basque

---

13 Coetzee, *Boyhood*, pp. 39–40, 47–8.

. . . Esperanto . . . Volapük' (CJ: 121). We are in a translated world with no clue to the original. This is the metaphysical status of this fiction, underived from a verifiable truth.

From the moment that Simón recognizes David's mother, he is subtly changing from reasonableness to a belief in the boy. In the matter of the boy's education, however, he still lingers in reason. He does not like the way Inés, the mother, is spoiling him, turning him into a 'little prince'. He constantly explains nature, human nature and the world that the boy must accept in order to go forward. But a series of looks into the boy's eyes, as he resists reading through learning to write, and resists the abstract idea of numbers, gives Simón brief epiphanies that start to shake him into the acceptance of an imagined access to an epistemology that might hold the Karoo of the absent narrating subject's dreams, elsewhere, not in a nation named 'South Africa', which can only dismiss such efforts.[14] He comes to understand magic as coexisting with daily life. But it is the acceptance by his brothers at work of his previous suggestion of bringing in technology that finally teaches him how to believe. The crane that is brought in swings, filled with grain, and hits him in the chest. He is in hospital close to death. It is in this condition that he has that vision of transfiguration I have quoted above. He comes to glimpse why the boy did not wish to read through learning to make letters and how he understands numbers:

14 Njabulo Ndebele's comradeship with 'J. M.' and Abiola Irele's careful readings shine out in this general gloom. (Personal correspondence with the author.)

When I was in hospital with nothing else to do, I
tried, as a mental exercise, to see the world through
David's eyes. Put an apple before him and what does
he see? An apple: not *one* apple, just *an* apple [. . .]
what is the singular of which *apples* is the plural?
Three men in a car heading for the East Blocks: who
is the singular of which *men* is the plural—[. . .] Are
we three, or are we one and one and one? [. . .] *how
shall I ever get from zero to one?* From nowhere to
somewhere: it seemed to demand a miracle each
time [. . .] What if this boy is the only one among us
with eyes to see? (CJ: 248–50)

In the real world, Melanie Klein had worked with the
thought that for the child, metaphors and abstractions are
real, and had guided her young patients into that real world.
In the world of Coetzee's imagining, 'is there anyone on earth
to whom numbers are more real?' (CJ: 248), and belief guides
this question away from a merely reasonable 'coming to his
senses' (CJ: 249).

When the boy writes miraculously, something makes
him write *Deos* (Greek) for *Dios* (Spanish), and *Yo soy la verdad*
for *Conviene que yo digo la verdad* (CJ: 218, 225). Earlier, Simón
had approached this sort of uncanny behaviour through
the idea of consubstantiation and had likened it to the philosophical belief associated with cannibalism (CJ: 171). He had
tried to grasp the 'natural' in the supernatural, the actuality
of flesh and blood rather than the Eucharist. But now, all differences fall away.

This is not an either-or. Literature is not evidence. It is an attempt to access an episteme within which, magical, the Christ-child can be imagined as real. It is an attempt to celebrate an axis where the childlike is not held as childish. An attempt to earn the right to lie down in the Karoo left behind. Simón cannot bring it to a conclusion, of course. The book ends with the sentence: 'Looking for somewhere to stay, to start our new life' (CJ: 277); almost, but not quite, the opening sentence—an iteration, a displacement, not a repetition; opening up to what Eugenio would call 'bad infinity' (CJ: 250)—a *mise en abyme*. We cannot know if his words to Inés—'I will follow you to the ends of the earth' are spoken— he pauses, resisting the words that want to come out—'I will follow you to the ends of the earth' (CJ: 263). Fiction as resisting the historical future, when the brotherhood of Simon Peter will 'civilize' primitive socialist bureaucratic patriarchies for colonialism.[15]

If we look at Barthes's mind-blowing essay, published in 1966, which took us away from the way we taught—'Introduction to the Structural Analysis of Narratives'—we will see that it is not about structuralist analysis. Barthes offers us a detailed tabulation of various functions in a text, which would operate well; but at the end of the essay, he undoes the whole

---

15 Rather than present a binary opposition between the supernatural and true religion: 'He [the African] is the very embodiment of Africa when she shall have lost her immemorial contacts with the Supernatural, unless she has a supreme God to lean on' (Jean K. Mackenzie [ed.], *Friends of Africa* [Cambridge, MA: United Study of Foreign Missions, 1928], p. 224; book in Du Bois's private collection; passage marked in pencil, presumably by him).

thing by interpreting the narrative function as simply the human obligation not to keep on repeating:[16] that the human being is an 'abnormal' blip in the sea of death—*thanatos* (Freud)—because the repetition automatism (Lacan) must be broken.

Reading theory for itself rather than for the immediate presentation of literature as evidence of theories, we also begin to move towards the named author Coetzee who has read these theories backward. What we as readers have to puzzle out is what is escaping this elaborately set theoretical ruse as the obvious desire of the text. It is hinted that the judgement of the Nobel Prize Committee was 'wrong', because *Disgrace* must be overwritten. We know that that story is broken in some way, but what are we going to do with that knowledge? And we know dates. Between the 1974 of *Dusklands* and the 1999 of *Disgrace* is the past of the text. This allows me to think Coetzee's chronology as author. I am grateful that I was taught to be a literalist. The bigger the author, the more simple-minded his tricks. The proof of the metanarratives and so forth is the surface. This is not a creative writing workshop. Coetzee is doing with theory what in jazz would be called a 'kinky rendition': just off the beat, setting up the theories, rather than proving them, as the early work of Zoë Wicomb would do. I take the hint to be literal. Located in South Africa earlier, he wrote about the white man

---

16 Roland Barthes, 'Introduction to the Structural Analysis of Narratives' in *Image Music Text* (Stephen Heath trans.) (London: Fontana, 1977), pp. 79–124; here, p.124.

after Independence. After he leaves South Africa, Coetzee begins to write about immigrants, starting with *Slow Man* (2005). In *Summertime*, the two are brought together. One of them in Canada, one of them going to the United States, one of them in Britain, one of them in Paris and one person in South Africa whose story is not yet finished. All the others are finished. The placing of Martin, the white man in England, is deliberately misplaced chronologically, a misplacement that we are invited to check. The reader is asked to do something with it, because the reader is asked to judge what has come before. This man is, textually, 'later'. The author-as-character represents the desire to revise, placed as a contrast to the anguish of Margot. We look at two different textualized desires.

Thus we have one 'locatable' and one 'fictive' character. Coetzee has constructed this combination. In this text, whoever the author is belongs to you as reader, as you belong to the author in all texts. What is the desire held in the text below this ruse of personality? That is the question with which we begin. The theory that is crowding into our heads as we read this obviously theoretical text is an invitation to the (im)possible task of active forgetfulness. It is helpful that we know that the 'actual author' is himself an English teacher and a major theorist. I want to go on to another text before we come back here.

I wrote a piece on Coetzee's *Foe* some time ago, on which his comment, if I remember right, was that I spoke his worst fears. Such a private communication can have its place in a reading such as this one, for it is part of how an author teaches us how (not) to read them. Coetzee is a man of great precision. You can take his comment as a piece of criticism. *Foe* is about colonialism. After that, in the middle, are texts about postcoloniality. *Summertime* is about immigrants. Margot, the only located person in this text, is the one about whom the autobiographical character is made to say, 'I am doing free indirect discourse,' so that there can be a distinction between what she says and the rest of the text. What is the function of this representation of metanarrative and heteroglossia? They are giving a certain kind of voice to the inhabitant of a particular section, as the book does what literature always does, but less obtrusively: it sets up a private value system. She is the only located person; it is the only part of the text that is really open. Coetzee's concerns share something with Lukács' description of Sancho Panza at the end of *Don Quixote*: he escapes the novel. Christophine in Rhys' *Wide Sargasso Sea* (1966) escapes the novel. These are important moments in novels, and these discussions frame the story about the German whom Lukas loathes and who offers a comment about South Africa. Coetzee makes Margot say something to Vincent, which Vincent writes in the indirect free discourse, emphasized in the text, which Margot does not contradict. She wants to spit in the German's eye but holds herself back.

We are being taught to read this textually by the novel itself: as half-empty—that literature is always constructed—or, half-full; that given that no book, no novel, can let you

'know' anything, this book, by manipulating that characteristic, through novelistic and rhetorical conduct, tries to give
a voice to that one character by locating her in place. Everything else is about immigration, including, after *Disgrace*, the
named author himself. That is what the novel literally is
'about', not a proof of 'postmodern theories' but a useful
negotiation with the literariness of literature and the possibility of attending to representation. This, at least, is the
desire of the text, even if necessarily unfulfilled.

I want to compare this to a nineteenth-century novel,
a novel of Chartism: *North and South* (1855) by Elizabeth
Gaskell. Chartism was an important movement that began
the possibility of strikes in the name of people's rights.
Engels read about Chartism, Marx engaged with the Chartists
in the establishment of the International Working Men's
Association, Rosa Luxemburg read about Chartism, Carlyle
wrote about Chartism, South African women wrote a charter
as these British workers had written a charter in the eighteenth century in Britain. Most liberals say Chartism was a
failure, as they say the 1905 Russian General Strike was a failure. But they are not failures if you take into account the way
they changed things, following, of course, the logic of the
future anterior.

Raymond Williams does not like the novel because the
female protagonist marries the man at the end.[17] He does not

17 Raymond Williams, 'The Industrial Novels' in *Culture and Society, 1780–
1950* (London: Penguin, 1961[1958]), pp. 87–109; here, pp. 102–3.

recognize that Mrs Gaskell is attempting to stage 'marriage' in a certain way. It is a novel that has gendering at its centre. As does *Summertime*. You cannot just talk about metanarratives here. It is about 'men's' anxiety: the anxiety of the man who is writing an autobiographical novel (Coetzee has used many female narrators from *The Age of Iron* on), trying to access the other, and that of the man who writes on women's novels, diagnosing. For Coetzee and Williams, straight guys trying to enter into all different kinds of female characters and authors, and for Coetzee, to imagine how they would describe him as a sexually unsatisfactory person, is not just about metanarratives (we could go to a moment in *Waiting for the Barbarians*).[18] This is the autobiographical topic: at once 'true' or 'correct' and deeply anxious statements. These kinds of things are never right or wrong. What, indeed, is the difference between virtue and the sustained pretence of virtue?

North and South, like a good political novel, is engaged in training the imagination of the reader. Indeed, we can expand this argument to other kinds of texts as well, if we learn how to read 'the literary': that is how we looked at Fanon teaching us about Hegel teaching us how to read Hegel. We are not talking general theories: we are talking about texts as teaching texts, teaching the reader how to read *this* text, not all texts.

In Mrs Gaskell's novel, you see a sign: a woman embracing a man—in a liminal space; not just because gender is liminal but because class is liminal as well. The space is a

18 J. M. Coetzee, *Waiting for the Barbarians* (New York: Penguin, 1980).

threshold between the factory and the factory owner's residence. At a time when the entire class structure of Britain is transiting from feudalism to capitalism, as indeed in Coetzee's novel, in which the time-transit is from colony to post-colony, apartheid to new nation, Mrs Gaskell's book is about the education of a working-class man who has risen into gentlemanliness to become a *malik* (a capitalist), as Coetzee's text is about how to be educated into effective postcoloniality. For Mrs Gaskell, the entire class system is becoming more fluid; as capital enters, aristocracy can no longer mean the same thing—as in Coetzee, citizenship, hence immigration. Thus, the liminal space is neither *ghor* nor *bahir*, as in Tagore's *Ghore Baire*—Inside (the home) and Outside.[19] It is the space where outside, the strikers are striking, and inside is the home of the capitalist. On the threshold, stand the two protagonists, the woman and the man. When the woman sees that the strikers are going to hit the man, she embraces him and takes the stone on her forehead.[20] She behaves like a human being rather than a woman. This is the character in the sense of a letter, an ideograph. The sign male-female, the matricial institution of being human, is being sign-ified differently. How do we understand this basic character of all humankind, the signifier of reproductive heteronormativity, a woman willingly embracing a man, *lajjaharan* (the taking away of shame), not just in the interest of marriage? This is

19 Rabindranath Tagore, *The Home and the World* (Sreejata Guha trans., Swagata Ganguli introd.) (New Delhi: Penguin, 2005).

20 Elizabeth Gaskell, *North and South* (Alan Shelston ed.) (New York: W. W. Norton, 2005), p. 163.

the lesson Williams cannot learn. The classical meaning of marriage, here, would be wrong. By making the woman marry the man, Gaskell does not behave like a single-issue feminist. Throughout the book, she dramatizes the misunderstanding of the new sign by everyone—the man as well as his mother, and even, of course, the self-doubting protagonist.

In the end, Mr Thornton, rather than learn to be a gentleman through instruction by the protagonist's doubting clergyman father, learns to be a 'socialist owner'. It is the idea of capital being turned for the use of the social, rather than only for capitalism, an early notion of sustainability. Whether we agree with this is not the question here. (Anybody who supports corporate social responsibility would be obliged to recognize more than a model here—a riff on social democracy.) The idea of Chartism in those early days was this. This is Engels. This is the idea that the emergence of capital has to be used in a socialist rather than a capitalist way, dictated by the needs of the proletariat. This is the lesson that Thornton learns through Margaret Hale, who is very friendly with the strikers. Gaskell makes one of the strikers, the leading person, bitterly rue the fact that another of the strikers had gone to violence, because one of the ideals of the General Strike which so appealed to bourgeois ideologues was, firstly, that the agent of the General Strike is the proletariat, and secondly, that the success of the General Strike does not, like extra-democratic regime change, assume violence. Violence comes from the other side, but they are wrong. (Gandhi will say that passive resistance is not a coward's way.)

The capital being used comes from the woman. Margaret inherits from Mr Bell, a Cambridge don, from feudal money, as it were. Mr Bell is a gentleman. (We should remember the distinction between gentleman and capitalist, a distinction that Vivek Chibber's recent book seems to ignore.)[21] I am making it into a very structured novel—it is not such a thing. It is a splendid, long novel written for serial publication in the 1850s. She says no to her would-be lawyer boyfriend who is now a banker and is advising her about the money. She takes it into her own hands and when all the banks have refused to finance Mr Thornton's 'socialist' project for running his enterprise, she finances him. That is the real end of the story. This is the mid-nineteenth century in Britain; so the novel is not talking about what happened to managerial labor in the twentieth century. We should not read it as such. It is being written by a clergyman's wife, a woman being mocked by Charles Dickens in his correspondence with his own editor, and being congratulated one-on-one.[22]

At the end of the book, Thornton and Margaret embrace again.[23] Although this is a private embrace, we have, by this point, been trained to read the master character of reproductive heteronormativity differently. Taking the stone in the

---

21 Vivek Chibber, *Postcolonial Theory and the Specter of Capital* (New York: Verso, 2013). I have written about this in greater length in 'Penny for the Old Guy', *Cambridge Review of International Affairs* 27(1) (2014): 184–98.

22 For Charles Dickens' correspondence with W. H. Wills, the sub-editor of his weekly magazine *Household Words* on the subject of *North and South*, see Gaskell, *North and South*, p. 412.

23 Ibid., p. 395.

forehead has been displaced into becoming the financer of running the socialist factory. They make a joke about class: how much their families would despise the fact that they are marrying. The novel is not all about gender, as is *Jane Eyre*, or all about class, as is *Hard Times* (1854).

If we go back to Coetzee's novel, we find that there are two tight embraces—just Julia and Margot. Let us keep in mind the alteration of signification in *North and South*. The first embrace reported in *Summertime* is from Coetzee to Julia. He hugs her incredibly tightly when she in the subjunctive says: 'If I were free, would you marry me?' (S: 64) J. M. Coetzee the author is representing something, either because it is true or because it is not true, but this does not depend upon its postmodern form. He is presenting it, which is all that matters. This depends on all discourse. This is why, for evidence, you have cross-examination. This is not evidence. He is presenting something either true or false, but he is presenting it, which is all that matters. This character, who is universally—according to Coetzee's stereotyped description of Coetzee through his attempt to imagine the other different kinds of women, not just one woman—taken to be unsuited for marriage. We cannot know; because in the text, we also have to think about the man who won the Nobel Prize. Therefore, *he* embraces, incredibly tightly, when she says: 'If I were free, would you marry me?'

The other side of that embrace comes from the woman in the Margot section. She embraces him very, very tightly and then writes that letter, the letter that is almost not sent.

Rhetorically, it is shown to be almost not sent, and in fact *it* is not sent, because the letter that is sent has an 'insincere' signature, as the text is careful to point out. A signature endorses a letter. The signature section of this letter does not endorse this letter's sincerity and the passionate mood of the sender. Why would Coetzee put in that gap? Perhaps to signal the break between the writing of that extraordinary letter and the sending of it:

> [B]y evening she is too exhausted to pursue the letter she was writing, and anyhow she has lost touch with the feeling. *Am thinking of you*, she writes at the foot of the page. Even that is not true, she has not given John a thought all day, she has had no time. *Much love*, she writes. *Margie*. She addresses the letter and seals it. So. It is done (S: 138).

The signature section that gives evidentiary plausibility and value to a communication is not represented as trustworthy here. I am just talking rhetorical conduct of the book round the repeated gendered sign of a man and a woman embracing. There are scenes of copulation and sexual intercourse, but these are not those. There is a difference being made between a social contract—marriage—and a scene of embrace which has been cleansed of any connection with prurience or physical passion. We have had scenes about good lovemaking and bad lovemaking. This is not that. What is this, then? We must linger with the question.

'After *Disgrace*,' says Sophie, 'I lost interest,' (S: 242) which is a way of saying, 'That's the interesting stuff.' It is a

colleague in Paris—someone least connected and most connected. I wrote a piece vindicating *Disgrace*, lamenting the African National Congress' withholding of reading. Other African writers have expressed to me their displeasure with this text. Coetzee is not interested in legitimizing by reversal, being the good white, consistently politically correct, as is Nadine Gordimer. In *Disgrace*, he tried to invite readerly counter-focalization by constructing an unreliable central character, resembling the actual Coetzee. A risky move, which misfired. In that text, the new white citizen is the lesbian daughter, intertextual between *King Lear* and *The Trial*, agreeing to bear the child of rape, because reproduction is generalized rape, after all. Like Mary Oraon, if you like. 'Perhaps that is what I must learn to accept. To start at ground level. With nothing. Not with nothing but. With nothing,' says Lucy,[24] echoing *King Lear*, also a father–daughter thing, with a difference.

Then he left. Then he began to look at the phenomenon of migration. *Slow Man* is the first book written after his departure. Sophie does not read after that, remember, so the reader is being asked to read it. Remember, Margot is before Julia. How do we know that? Not through Martin. There is the ring-like autonormativity of the date there too. It is the date of Coetzee being refused a green card in the United States. It was in 1971 that Coetzee came back and Margot's story began. Julia's story is 1974, when *Dusklands* comes out. Why is it arranged this way? One reason from the conduct of

24 J. M. Coetzee, *Disgrace* (New York: Penguin, 1999), p. 205.

the rhetoric that I can imagine is: so that the embrace with Julia can be placed textually before the embrace with Margot, although it is sequentially after, and it should be arranged in such a way that it can be noticed by the canny literal-minded reader. The reader will notice why, because *Dusklands* came out in 1974, and he left America in 1971—Coetzee's biography is right there. The genre of the text is the ability to hold on to how one is judged by the other—female protagonists of various kinds—in terms of a gendered male. That is the first one. The second one is the issue of race. In *Disgrace*, the race issue seems inconsequential to strong lesbian gendership. Here, there is no such quick conclusion.

I would like to propose that *Summertime* is (and there will be more, because the Margot section is unfinished) a rewriting of *Disgrace*, making the persona of the located South African who wants to claim South Africa as also his country a different one. Not the incredibly difficult heroic Lucy, who is claiming the child of rape and saying that one must begin with nothing—we cannot be like her—and certainly not David Lurie, who is an unreliable narrator. Here, the author-function is put aside, but not let go as in *Disgrace*, in favour of an older technique of unreliable narrator, that bad readers cannot notice. Here, the author-function is present, and everyone is in character.

Indeed, what does he do in this novel that is different from both *Disgrace* and *Dusklands*? The embrace(s) has happened, we are moving along with the rhetoric, we who know how to read, being very literal-minded. We are seeing that there is the 'she' and the 'I' and so forth, and we are noticing the distance created between Vincent, who is the author-biographer persona, and Margot. Vincent is putting words in Margot's mouth as she says: 'You are really going too far. I said nothing remotely like that. You are putting words of your own in my mouth' (S: 119). Her mother goes to hospital; and before that, the Coetzee character speaks to her in an open kind of way (S: 133). We as readers keep noticing that the text is full of obvious falsehoods: nothing about his own wife and children, nothing about his own mother, the incorrect judge-ment when Adriana says: 'I know he won a big reputation later; but was he really a great writer?' (S: 195). Adriana is incorrect because she has never heard of Keats.

Here is the dialogue, Coetzee writing. He: 'I want to be able to be alone when I choose' (S: 133). And then she, really understanding him in a certain way: *'Best to cut yourself free of what you love, he had said during their walk—Cut yourself free and hope the wound heals.* She understands him exactly. That is what they share above all' (S: 134). He is not talking here about male and female but merely speaking about South Africa. 'That is what they share above all.' He is not being made to say it but she is allowed to say this through the use of the free indirect discourse. Free indirect discourse is given to the Coetzee figure by the text; and to this figure, by Vin-cent. That is a rhetorical way of giving voice in the literary text which is using, like a magician, the postmodern material, and Volosinov. 'That is what they share above all: not just a love of this farm, this *kontrei*, this Karoo'—Afrikaans entering only here. Coetzee is a Boer name. They insist they have always spoken English, but they are Boers and there is Afrikaans in the text:

> This is what they share above all: not just a love of this farm, this *kontrei*, this Karoo, but an understanding that goes with the love, an understanding that love can be too much. To him and to her it was granted to spend their childhood summers in a sacred space. That glory can never be regained; best not to haunt old sites, and come away from them mourning what is for ever gone (S: 134).

All the metanarrative stuff would go to waste if you think that this is Coetzee writing, because the white Creole may not have the right to say this. It was also not the white Creole writing in *Disgrace*, but because of the choice of the rhetorical instruments, the mistake was easier to make.

Njabulo Ndebele, who used to work with Steve Biko and was the first black vice chancellor of the University of Cape Town, feels that a country does not change simply with the change in the law, which is, of course, welcome. That is my entire point about education and the practice of freedom through intellectual labour. South Africa is still a place holder, as India is a place holder for people of colour in the United States. In the US census, we used to be 'Caucasian' (read, 'white'). When Lyndon Johnson lifted the alien registration quota in 1965, Indians became 'other'. My friend Kenneth Prewitt officiated in the two previous US censuses. The other day, he began to tell me: 'Oh Gayatri, you know, by the way, about Indians, about their slot in the US census.' I said, 'Ken, stop right there, I'll tell you.' This is the sort of thing that is going on here. The white Creole who loves the country as a sacred space, not very learned, but not a fool, does say this but does not have the right to say this. It is, therefore, placed in free indirect discourse third person—a third person who has been, pointedly, enabled in the text.

We can ask the question by way of Aparna Sen's film *36 Chowringhee Lane* (1981), a film about Eurasian Indians. Does the white Creole have the right to feel that South Africa is a sacred space? Being wary of loving too much is not something that makes sense to Lukas. You see why this love is not related to sexual intercourse. The line, 'With this body I thee worship,' which she quotes in terms of her sexuality with Lukas, comes from the Book of Common Prayer. Then she says that she cannot imagine her cousin giving himself wholeheartedly to anyone. Again, remember, this is Coetzee writing about 'Coetzee'. Every woman says something like this about that character. Always a quantum held back, held in reserve. After lunch they say their goodbyes. When John's turn comes, she 'hugs him tight, feeling his body against her tense, resistant' (S: 134–5), and then she goes back to the kitchen and she writes: 'They say you don't know a person properly until you have spent a night with him (or her)' (S: 135) and she talks about the fact that they had talked about marriage, et cetera.

We have, then, this particular scene of loving South Africa. Then, on page 140, the question of being allowed to feel this love comes up again, or are we supposed to say, like Lucy: I will accept the child of rape and begin with nothing but, but nothing. That is why *Disgrace* is still there. She does not like the new post office, because she likes her memory of the old post office. On the next page, she gives a description of her own letter, however cowardly. *'What are we doing here?*: that had been the unspoken question all the time. He had known it and she had known it' (S: 140). This is a very serious question: this *is* Coetzee's question. This is why Coetzee left, because he saw that it was not possible for him to be, in fact, an honest white Creole who can represent the situation. He dismisses the German who expresses that opinion in a very superficial way, who says: 'Beautiful country, beautiful landscapes, rich resources, but, many, many problems. How you will solve them I cannot see. In my opinion things will get worse before they will get better' (S: 144)—how many people have I heard say this about South Africa, coming and going? Coetzee makes Margot say this in the third person, given to her by Vincent, and here she does not contradict Vincent. This non-contradiction is the law of truth, the principle of non-contradiction. When Margot does not contradict Vincent the character, as she does elsewhere, we are supposed to give to that moment of non-contradiction the emphatic register of the veridical, within the limits of the fiction. Therefore, this is a way of rusing into a kind of 'true' position within a novel. The non-contradiction of the given, accepted indirect free discourse—Flaubert's gift to humankind. So, this is what Klaus the German says, that Margot says in the third person, reported by Vincent, whom she does not contradict. 'Lukas detests his brother-in-law,' and 'she would like to spit in his eye, but does not.' These are details that we read within the space of representation to come to a conclusion about the right of the white Creole to love South Africa as sacred space.

We should speak also of prayer, which is the beginning of the book. Before Margot talks to the 'Coloured' folks, Aletta and Johannes, she 'says': 'She would have liked to buy the two of them a cup of coffee at the café, would have liked to sit down with them in a normal, friendly way, but of course one could not do that without causing a fuss. *Let the time come soon, O Lord*, she prays to herself, *when all this apartheid nonsense will be buried and forgotten*' (S: 145). Margot has said before that she does not really believe in God, and she says prayer as a form is not a bad thing. A form—a rhetorical form. Then she goes on to talk about what she wants to say. She hopes for her words to be understood in their widest sense. After Coetzee the author of *Disgrace* makes her say 'young Coloured nurse named Aletta', thus putting us in as reader, we follow his signals as we are reading:

> 'I must tell you how much you and Johannes are doing for us', she says to Aletta. Aletta smiles back in the friendliest of ways, with not the faintest trace of irony. She hopes for her words to be understood in their widest sense, with all the meaning that for very shame she cannot express: *I must tell you how grateful I am for what you and your colleague are doing for an old white woman and her daughter, two strangers*

*who have never done anything for you but on the con-
trary have participated in your humiliation, in the land
of your birth, day after day after day. I am grateful for
the lesson you teach me through your actions in which
I see only human kindness, and above all through that
lovely smile of yours* (S: 145).

Then she also looks at how the whites, although there is
a subaltern white there, are kept in anti-subalternity. This is
completely unlike *Disgrace*, because Lucy *is* subalternized
there. '*Is it only we whites who are rushed by ambulance to a hospital—only the best!—where well-trained surgeons will sew our
fingers back on or give us a new heart as the case may be, and all
at no cost? Let it not be so, O Lord, let it not be so!*' (S: 146) Notice
another thing: within the indirect free discourse in italics, it
is a *we*. Coetzee is using typography. He is using this reported
speech technique to secure a fragile insecure place within
unverifiable discourse which will be a place of truth as it can
be in a literary text, which is not like evidence.

Coming to the end of this, there is a description of the
farm, where they are not making money because of the way
they run it. Next she is shown to make a mistake about John
Coetzee writing a best-seller and making lots of money—
slightly cheap irony. At the very end, John says, '"She won't
know me"' (S: 149)—a non-recognition sentence. This is
written somewhat in code for, 'She' is a shifter, the subject of
free indirect discourse. The last sentence which, within Coetzee's text, the biographer guarantees: 'It seems a good place.
She won't know me: a good line. [Silence.] Well, what is your

verdict?' (S: 152; brackets in the original). The '[Silence]' is turned round here, because generally the '[Silence]' comes from Vincent. If the reader is looking at the detail of the rhetorical conduct of the use of reported speech in this text, she sees that the position is reversed in this section. She is the one who is going to say something, and she is silent. '[Silence.] Well, what is your verdict? *My verdict? I still don't understand.*' She says this so that 'Vincent' can be made to say, 'You were part of your cousin. He was part of you. That is plain enough, surely. What I am asking is, can it stand as it is?'

We are drawn to that last line: 'She won't know me.' It is repeated once. 'She' is a shifter, although it does refer obviously to an antecedent, to the sick woman. But the female character has been endowed with an important place of justice, as it were. The reader cannot know how indirect and broad to make that short declarative sentence—there will be no recognition for me—and the general shifter character, 'she', cannot stand for humankind. Or can it? 'It', 'she', 'the land', 'he', 'that person' won't know me—there is no recognition here. Can that stand? This person who becomes the rewritten voice of the non-intellectual, non–Nobel Prize–winning representation by Coetzee as a figure of his desire? This is not evidence either of a theory or of South African politics. This is the laying out of a desire. This is an alternative person to whom this represented character, a named character with a date of birth, and here a date of death which is not specified, and the dates of the publication of two books, and the date of the Nobel Prize, asks: 'Can it stand as it is?'

The answer is: '*Not as it is, no. I want to go over it again, as you promised*' (S: 152), says this alternative voice, the voice that is allowed to say she knew him and they shared a childhood in the sacred space of the Karoo. I think this answer is also promise of future work. This is a certain kind of end of the text. Now we begin to get primed for reading, as it were. We begin to get the others.

In this reading, I have wanted my reader to see that this extremely noticeable use of technique is a way to bring him/her into the text and see what the technique is doing. I wanted to look at the sign posts set up so that you can go forward towards a very available biography, and I wanted to present the text as telling us how to read those two characters of man embracing woman, woman embracing man. Further, through the use of the many variations on indirect free discourse, the place of Margot as a kind of 'I' place, place of non-contradiction, creating a fragile and temporary place of truth, which finally then does not allow the admission of non-recognition from the 'she' as the appropriate end: 'Can it stand as it is?'—'No, not as it is.' But this is not the end of the book. It is just a certain kind of end. We go next into something else, from here.

QUESTIONS

1. Deconstruction

I never really learnt to do what Derrida did. I used to go to his lectures till the end to look at the moves he made and I was always surprised. I just read. If it looks like deconstruction, then that is up to someone else to say. Deconstruction these days is understood as a sexy word for analysis, dismantling, breaking up. That is not what it is supposed to describe. It does not really matter, I am not the language police. Language has its own way; it goes whatever way it goes. What *Summertime* is doing, I think, is desperately using certain resources in the handling of language that are available to a very adroit user of language, who is also presented as an incapable English teacher by the next section. There is irony here. The author is using the resources offered by rhetoric, not even language, to create a space which will seem to stand for 'truth'. All texts, after all, create value systems.

I will come back to *King Lear*. This is something that Tarak Nath Sen taught us: there is this huge rhetorical extravagance (Tarak-babu's phrase) at the beginning of the play, after which Lear turns towards Cordelia and says: 'Speak.' Cordelia says: 'Nothing, my lord.' Since iambic pentameter was rendered more regularly on the Elizabethan stage, rather than as the failed prose that is convention now, you have in that line, six syllables of silence. So, Lear says: 'Nothing?' Eight syllables of silence. Cordelia says: 'Nothing.' Eight syllables of silence, and then Lear says: 'Nothing will come of nothing: speak again.'[25] What Tarak-babu taught us is that, generally speaking, it is language that creates an impression, but that here, because Shakespeare is such an adroit user of language, he is using the silence to make the viewer understand the import of this encounter as theatre.

25 William Shakespeare, *King Lear* (R. A. Foakes ed.), The Arden Shakespeare Third Series (Walton-on-Thames: Nelson, 1997), 1.1.87–90.

This kind of thing is also happening in this text. Coetzee is using the resources of rhetoric by doing cartwheels on 'he', 'they', 'she', 'I within she', non-contradiction of the she-ness by putting the contradictions there, to show that she is not there and so on—he is making these moves to create a platform to launch the text. Deconstruction is precisely not taking everything away and breaking everything apart. What people forget is that there is a C-O-N in the middle of that word, because Derrida was redoing Heidegger's idea of *Destruktion*. Titles like *Deconstruction and Reconstruction of . . .* are, from this point of view, just the tiniest bit embarrassing.

That is what it means to say that the text lays out a desire to tell the truth. I had TB—I was touched by tuberculosis, so I have lost all my bronchial tubes. In the same way, if you are touched by deconstruction, the importance of the difficulty of telling the truth becomes absolutely plangent, because it is not an exposure of error, simply a careful consideration of the fragility and responsibility of producing something that will be in place, recognizable as 'truth'. What were we just told? That it will happen again: 'Can it stand as it is? *Not as it is, no.*' Coetzee is already securing that voice. It is as I have said before *Dusklands* and *Disgrace*. After *Disgrace*, it is about people who left South Africa for one reason or another, including himself. Why did he leave? '"She won't know me."' This one who is located, who is then presented as not at all Lucy but the ordinary white person who wonders, '*What are we doing here?*', good-hearted, wants to be nice, thanks you for being nice and so on. But history is also larger than personal goodwill, so this is not Coetzee, just as Lucy was not Coetzee.

You have asked a good question but my analysis is not a deconstruction of anything. All texts lay out desires. Some make it their topic. All texts can give you the practices of the ethical reflexes. Some texts represent those practices. This text represents the desiring character, about whom truth can be told because he is dead.

2. Readerly and Writerly / Detective Stories

Let me repeat myself: this text is not an example of a theoretical situation. It is what Barthes talks about when he says 'readerly' and 'writerly'. You cannot really go beyond Barthes's distinction of readerly and writerly, because Richard Miller, for some reason, did not translate *lisible* and *scriptible* as the readable and the writable, as he should have.[26] It is a wrong

26 Barthes writes: '[L]e texte scriptible est un présent perpétuel, sur lequel ne peut se poser aucune parole *conséquente* (qui le transformerait, fatalement, en passé); le text scriptible, c'est *nous en train d'écrire*, avant que le jeu infini du monde (le monde comme jeu) ne soit traversé, coupé, arrêté, plastifié par quelque système singulier (Idéologie, Genre, Critique) qui en rabatte sur la pluralité des entrées, l'ouverture des réseaux, l'infini des langages. Le scriptible, c'est le romanesque sans le roman, la poésie sans le poème, l'essai sans la dissertation, l'écriture sans le style, la production sans le produit, la structuration sans le structure. Mais les textes lisibles? Ce sont des produits (et non des productions), ils forment la masse énorme de notre littérature' (*S/Z* [Paris: Éditions du Seuil, 1970], p. 11).

Richard Miller's translation reads: 'The writerly text is a perpetual present, upon which no *consequent* language (which would inevitably make it past) can be superimposed; the writerly text is *ourselves writing*, before the infinite play of the world (the world as function) is traversed, intersected, stopped, plasticized by some singular system (Ideology, Genus, Criticism) which reduces the plurality of entrances, the opening of networks, the infinity of languages. The writerly is the novelistic without the novel, poetry

translation, not just a mistaken one. It took away the point Barthes makes that the text that cannot be read by us is the one that is getting written. Miller's wrong translation allowed the English readership to think that, for Barthes, the writerly text was simply a text that does not settle 'an ultimate meaning'. But, of course, that may be the definition of all texts if you think of the future anterior. Therefore, the idea of 'going beyond' the readerly–writerly distinction is, I believe, not available in the French. It is a limit that marks irreducibly the limits of the intending subject as reader.

The readable text is: 'I am giving a lecture. Coetzee has published a book. We have heard two papers. There have been questions, there have been answers, all in a language which we understand.' But in this room, each of us is alive and dying at the same time. Our bodies are at least producing urine all the time, whatever the hell else they are producing. All of the hormones are working inside our bodies non-stop, doing all kinds of things. Glucose is being released, et cetera. The psychobiographies of our parents and their parents and their parents are also at work in the way in which our genes have been constituted and so on and so forth. All of this is happening. This is the writable. I have taken the most important, inaccessible examples but many more can be given. In the 70s, the inheritors of bourgeois humanism, with their

without the poem, the essay without the dissertation, writing without style, production without product, structuration without structure. But the readerly texts? They are products (and not productions), they make up the enormous mass of our literature' (Roland Barthes, *S/Z* [Richard Miller trans.] [London: Jonathan Cape, 1975], p. 5).

excess of access to the bourgeois world, said that while you read what you read, a text is getting written that is a much more important text. The planet is getting closer to its death. Huge figures are moving in outer space. We are not falling off, but time is moving.

Anish Kapoor's extraordinary sculpture, *My Red Homeland* (2003), is a great red circle on which a black dial moves second by second. If you stand in front of it, you cannot see any movement. You come back 15 minutes later and the dial has moved a good deal. It is like a clock, nothing unusual, except it makes you more aware of it. That is the writable. The writable has no end. It writes itself almost like a player piano or any digital equivalent. You cannot read it. You might say that electronic capital is writable. The old idea of realizing and the transformation of money into capital and the like has been revised because of the virtual material that never gets real-ized, as well as the whole cloud of capital, as it were: not only does this virtual material not get real-ized but it does not really enter into the calculations either, because it is moving so fast. That is the writable and it is also getting written as we are sitting here. Foreign exchanges are rising and falling. You can catch a moment of it as readable but not the entire abstract movement. That is also the new writable.

Barthes also talks about the desire expressed by writers like Alain Robbe-Grillet, who were trying to represent the inaccessibility of the writer by undermining the place of the intending readerly subject in the text. Actually, the desire to catch the writable is a pervasive human desire. If we want specifically noticeable examples, one of the most glorious spoofs of this desire is of course *Tristram Shandy* (1759)!

We can think of the text as a detective novel. You have to work it out, e-labor-ate it. In fact, the entire theoretical method of Deleuze and Derrida and Foucault can be seen in this way—perhaps, once again, textuality, always there for transactional e-labor-ation, is like that.

3. Intertextual Moments

On page 4 of *Summertime*, there is '*Agenbite of inwit*', a Middle English phrase which means prick of conscience—the intelligence inside us pricks again and again. It is a Christian homily to which Joyce also refers in *Finnegans Wake* (1939). Such allusions are appropriate to the English teacher. On page 33, 'How sweetly flows that liquefaction of her clothes.' That, too, seems not very much more than an English literature teacher's reflex and may indeed be there to mark the difference between the author-function and Julia, who is not placed within the English literary tradition acquired by the Boer, John Coetzee. On the other hand, Julia Frankl, a former student of German literature, does 'use' a German reference with greater adroitness as part of her remembered discussion of books with John Coetzee the author. Kafka's much-quoted youthful letter to Oskar Pollak, his childhood friend, gives us the definition of a book as a weapon of violent epistemological change and this is what Julia is made to offer to John, who seems to have, if her memory is veridical (as Vincent must think), a more conventional self-representation of what he desired from his own writings.[27] The passage may even invite the reader to think how biographical 'facts' are produced. Fact versus fiction, again.

In this novel, intertextuality works at the surface of the text, given for the canny reader to help in the process of evaluating veridicality by its private grammar. The more of these references you catch, the more you are becoming the implied reader of the text, as it were. By contrast, in *Disgrace*, the entire meaning of the entire text is braided together with the majesterial inter-texts. In other words, intertextuality as a technique can be used differently, and in my reading of *Disgrace*, I was only offering the explanation that we used to call 'deep allusions', as we learnt it in college, like 'As the wakeful bird / Sings darkling' in Milton going to Keats, 'Darkling I listen', and then to Hardy's 'The Darkling Thrush'. Or Keats' 'Thou still unravish'd bride of quietness' to Yeats' 'Upon the brimming water among the stones'. Deep allusions enhance the meaning. In *Summertime*, trying to undo David Lurie, Coetzee undermines intertextuality itself as no more than a surface tool to catch veridicality or 'trustworthiness' in terms of what the text can report, perhaps because *Disgrace* had been read as if it were a reprehensible but trustworthy expression of the author's sentiments about race.

---

27 'A book must be the axe for the frozen sea inside us' (Franz Kafka, *Letters to Friends, Family and Editors* [Beverly Colman, Nahum N. Glatzer, Christopher J. Kuppig and Wolfgang Sauerland eds, Richard and Clara Winston trans] [London: Oneworld Classics, 2011(1977)], p. 16).

This technique is almost absent in the Margot sections, perhaps because there is no reason for the reader to take on the role of a participant in evaluating her. It will happen with Adriana; it certainly happens with Julia. And, it happens consistently with John Coetzee; again, the undoing of David Lurie, showing how fiction undoes fact in order to deliver 'truth' and its production.

TEACHING AND AUTOBIOGRAPHY

The papers given at this last session draw forth from me some comments on the history and diversity of my scenes of teaching. For the last 60 years and more, we have been reading excellent criticism about how, in spite of its capitalization, we should not take Paris as representative of France. In the outside world, however, scholars take Delhi to be a metonymic representative of India as a monolith. This has a reverse effect on papers produced from the two elite universities located in Delhi. They come to resemble papers produced from a generic United States. We have to keep this in mind as part of Fanon's criticisms of the metropolitan immigrant. Here we are discussing an immigrant who is not an immigrant, as it were—generalized 'US' discourse emerging in a distant capital city where the conditions of life are altogether different as well. We should take this as the narrative of the writing of criticism itself to be an ethical instantiation.

My scene of teaching began in Calcutta in 1959—if I discount the earlier class-hatched scenes of forcing domestic

In the class, Spivak's remarks were preceded by presentations by Santosh Maholkar and Aruni Mahapatra, MPhil students at the Department of English, University of Pune. These papers are available upon request.

servants of various ages to become 'literate' when I was myself pre-teen, encouraged by my mother's invitation to me to participate in grading the many, many papers that came from Hiranmoyee Bidhaba Shilpashram—an institute for making destitute widows employable. In 1959, I transformed the stereotype of myself as a more marketable commodity by learning an 'English' accent—and thus began teaching in a way that did not involve reproducing myself: Mr Murakami, the Japanese executive from Mitsubishi, a well-paying English conversation student, being the most extreme example. In 1964, when I was a teaching assistant, the implicit racial profiling by the students kept some species of difference intact. It all changed when, in 1965, I became an assistant professor at a university devoted to the ideas of the 60s: everything in the humanities must conform to the students' desires.

I believe it was a disaster. I turn instead to the insight in Marx's third thesis on Feuerbach (published in 1888), which argues that between teacher and taught, there must always be a difference in experience and knowledge which the teacher must always attempt to overturn (*Umwälzung*—overturning, not 'revolution' as in the English translation). The unsupported anxiety of students in the 60s in the United States at specific universities—identifying revolution itself with a declaration of 'I want' everywhere and the concurrent accusations of teachers as definitively engaged in power play—destroyed the possibility of education to an extent, whereas Marx, in his third thesis, insists on the education of the educators:

The materialist doctrine that men are products of circumstances and upbringing, and that, therefore, changed men are products of other circumstances and changed upbringing, forgets that it is men that change circumstances and that the educator himself needs educating. Hence, this doctrine necessarily arrives at dividing society into two parts, of which one is superior to society (in Robert Owen, for example.)

The coincidence of the changing of circumstances and of human activity can be conceived and rationally understood only as *overturning practice*.[1]

Not only is Delhi a metonym for India, but its self-representation as India is also deeply troublesome. It has become, like Istanbul today (for a different reason that I cannot elaborate here today), a Seminar City, its universities holding beautifully organized seminars, like those in Bei-Da or Tsing-hua. Drifting representations of 'the US', unmoored to the specific socius.

In India, this Delhi-problem was noticeable in Kerala last year. One of the characteristics of the typical US paper at the universities where I have taught is the length of time taken up with a description of the writer's inability to give a paper. This is a topos. I discourage my students from that sort of navel-gazing.

1 Karl Marx, 'Theses on Feuerbach (III)' in *Karl Marx and Frederick Engels: Selected Works*, VOL. 2 (Moscow: Foreign Languages Publishing House, 1962), pp. 403–4, translation modified.

The literary text is not an illustration of the theories of Barthes (round whom there seems to be a kind of *guruvada*). It is also not an illustration of Coetzee's essay on autobiography in 1984. *Feu la cendres*—fire ash—is a representation, in Derrida, of relationship without relationship, *rapport sans rapport*. The relationship between justice and law, gift and responsibility, is such a relationship, marked by non-access— a rewrite of Kant's transcendental deduction. I leave this as a hint here for the reader to develop, simply adding that in Kant, it is a correction of Locke who, according to Kant, wishes to produce evidence back to the origin of an argument.

In Derrida, ash is a testimony and witnessing of the fact of fire, a trace of the possibility that the gift becomes not just responsibility but even accountability, reckoning; that inde-constructible justice can only be accessed as revisable law. When the poet says: *Ki pai ni tari hishab milatey mono mor nahey raji*—my mind does not agree to balance the account of what I have not received—it is a statement of a desire to be in control of a decision to deny the limit to one's power.

One of the papers interestingly suggested that there is an attempt in *Summertime* at textualizing the life. The next question, then, is: Where does life begin? How textual already is 'life' as we think we know it? The Euro-US writers who gave us 'intentional fallacy' had a pre-critical notion of life as a series of brute facts, as opposed to the text. Or is it that the many-strandedness, wovenness of a life asks us to undo that opposition? It was a permission to let the authors carry what-ever stated political position as permitted by the narrative of communism versus freedom and let the written text—text in the narrow sense—stand free. As we have noticed, Derrida does not acknowledge this in either Nietzsche or Heidegger.

Literature tells us how not to generalize. We must wait to be surprised. Therefore, the fact that within a text that was written in 1984, where Coetzee is writing as a writer-critic, there may be remarks about biography and autobiography which must not stop us from welcoming the contingent from long after in *Summertime*. And, of course, ultimately, you do not need to read *Summertime*, or anything. We are within an English Department, and departmental requirements make you read texts and write on texts. Let us not forget this fact. Within that framework, you must make the reading match the theoretical sophistication. And that sophistication must not make the writer's self-representation contaminated by vanity.

We must have enough distance from the intending subject to be able to look at the signals given by a literary text; that is the substance of reading, the more literal the better.

Let us now come back to the idea of South Africa in *Summertime*. Looking at textual signals, I was saying that the reason why Sophie is made to say what she says is to throw emphasis on what she cannot read. Also, that the reader must understand the importance of the heterogeneity of the author-function by noticing the distinction between 'J. M. Coetzee' and 'John Coetzee'. Not only is it all stage-managed but in the stage management, Coetzee is also using an old rule of narration. Each of these utterances comes from a character, and we must place their trustworthiness in terms of how the character has been itself staged in the text.

Coetzee is also making these characters representative of certain positions. Julia Smith/Frankl is in the diagnosis business and she is put first. We identify first with this diagnosing character as we read *Summertime*. It is as if the 'author as a sign' (Barthes), and the author's 'subject position' (Foucault) are being negotiated through this character. Coetzee took his PhD at the University of Texas, and the best teachers there were learning from structuralism on how to do and how not to do African studies, anthropology and the humanities in general. Therefore, what we are looking at in *Summertime* may be the structuralist imperative to say that the subject position is the subject that emerges from the behaviour of the structures. Every statement has its contradiction in the book. It is a teaching text of the double bind. The 'author' says: I'm absent, I'm absent, I'm absent—but it is part of the technique. It is the textualizing of a life, the inscription of a desire to be able to access a life. In the end, we discover that the novel is 'notes towards' a novel. And that is a topos. We are invited to read as we read Gramsci's prison journals, or Proust's *In Search of Lost Time* (1922–31).

How do we know that? Through the notes at the end of the sections that are from the man represented as the dead man. The notes say: 'To be developed', et cetera. It has been emphatically said that the person who wrote these is dead. That is a textual event, not just a narrative event. That means it is an open text. It is the representation of the inaccessible writerly. The writing of the writable is done by no intending person. This is why Nietzsche described us many years ago as strapped to the back of the tiger—which is our body, which we cannot really know, except for very crude signals.

This desire, to represent the writable that is beyond our control, is shared by all of us. Women and the subaltern classes have been denied the right to represent the writable. Their social task is to manage the readable—the family, and, in this text, 'Marion be good', and all that it implies. At the end of his 'structural analysis' essay, Barthes calls this desire to represent the writable part of the human programming of breaking what in his day would be called the pre-human obligation to repeat, not to be merely part of the writable. And, because of the representation of the desire to represent the writable, this text, rather ostentatiously, has no closure. Lukács defined *Don Quixote* as the first modern novel.[2] In the character of Sancho Panza, it represented the desire to 'give over the text to the world', a variation on the desire to represent the writable. This does not mean that these texts, in fact, can organize their own non-closure, because, as texts, they are also bound in their very desire for freedom.

Therefore, in my reading, the representation of John Coetzee as dead is part of the representation of the desire to control the writable.

Some representations of the desire to represent the writable are more aggressive than others. Even *North and*

2 See György Lukács, *The Theory of the Novel* (Anna Bostock trans.) (Monmouth: Merlin, 1971), particularly, 'The Romanticism of Disillusionment', pp. 112–31.

South, a realistic novel, interrupts the massive closure of boy-
meets-girl with a reference to the openness of class. And
indeed, in every text, in the text of life, there is no closure—
the future is undecidable, and dead we push up the daisies.

And, in fact, real non-closure is not in our hands. We
give birth to our own death, as Richard Dawkins and other
writers about DNA tell us. Their main point is that only a very
small percentage of DNA is used by the human being and
most of it is just passed on over trillions of years before the
beginning or after the end of humanity. We are instruments
for the passing on of DNA. We are birthing machines for the
passage of DNA. No closure. At the other extreme is Melanie
Klein, for whom birth itself is a kind of dying, because uter-
ine life is opened up in the shock and trauma of what we
normally think of as birth into life. The trauma of birth is
not something that one forgets: we must endure our going
hence, as we endure our coming hither. 'Ripeness is all.'[3]
Ripeness, like the cucumber in the mourning chant—burst-
ing to deposit its seeds into the soil and thus to continue into
death beyond closure.[4] This is intertextuality.

We are looking at representation. If there are languages
where the resources of representation are not identical, we
do not make immediate social claims dependent on the
nature of the resources.

We do not, for example, say: 'Since in Bengali, there is
no gender for the nouns,' because it is a more elaborated

[3] Shakespeare, *King Lear*, 5.2.11.
[4] See also Gayatri Chakravorty Spivak, 'Thinking about Edward Said: Pages
from a Memoir', *Critical Inquiry* 31(2) (Winter 2005): 519–25.

language, which simply means 'in use', 'therefore it shows that Bengalis are without gender discrimination.' Hema Malini said in New York that Hinduism is wonderful because it has goddesses, and Hindus like women. That is also a piece of complete zero. We must not monumentalize a language as social index. In *Summertime*, only academics—Martin and Sophie—are allowed to summarize. When we quote Sophie, we must keep this in mind. The two academics come after the serious texts of the two women. We are told something about the text's valuation of academics by Martin's clearly incorrect, shallow, rhetorical question: 'Will it amount to anything more than—forgive me for putting it this way—anything more than women's gossip?' (S: 218). Martin is not in the spirit of the text but he is in the business of using a socially recognizable technique of representing truth: academic summary. This is a short-cut representation of truth through non-contradiction, which Martin and Sophie, in their different ways, share.

On the other hand, the woman at the centre of the book, placed within free indirect discourse, contradicts, saying, 'You're not saying what I said,' so that when she does not say this, if we are noticing and reading carefully—all of that is protected by an invisible, expansive and perhaps even 'in-depth' non-contradiction. It is not truth that the fiction offers but rather a set of textual instructions for the rhetorical discovery of the universally acknowledged way of locating the characteristics of 'truth': A is not B; A is A. When this goes on indefinitely and 'without closure', it is a *mise en abyme*, a hall of mirrors, an abyssality. We must remember that this is not being done for its own sake, to dazzle us technically. My reader's instinct, right or wrong, suggests that the 'truth'-s that are being approached by these diversified and abyssal fictive measures go towards answering difficult historical questions such as: Who can say the truth about the place of the colonial in space? Space belongs to no one. Where does colonialism begin and end? When does it end? I remember Samir Amin in 1973 making new suggestions about the historical narrative as, in 1966, Barthes had about narrative as such. Amin's idea was that it was the movement of people rather than mode of production alone that wrote history. It is within these two stalwarts that I place today the struggle for which there was a pre-given end product: national liberation. That fell into the uncomfortable fact that the world is not owned by anyone and that capital has no country. It is no use saying that the whites were unkind to us. We were also unkind, historically and now. Therefore, there is no truth but in fiction.

This is why we have to remember that this novel is not just for showing off the literary, or becoming an illustration of certain kinds of theories. It is in use, to present, and for the reader to represent, the tough problem of 'does the good white guy . . .' It applies to us! The upwardly mobile people from other groups are always open to accusations, and only sometimes correctly, by a too-simple, unexamined identity politics. You do not have the right because you *are* not this. As a human being with one life, what is the burden of history for the white Creole? Or the socio-critical caste Hindu? Was Marx just a bourgeois ideologue? These are questions that one covers over by only being nice to the blacks as a faceless group—a legitimation by reversal of racism. In the anteroom of the Museum of Modern Art in New York, there is a small sculpture, which is simply a *mise en abyme*: two mirrors reflecting back and forth. Those questions are also represented by this box. Who wins, loses. But then, who loses, wins—and it is always possible that losing is better than winning. It is the bad leaders and politicians who think there is a winning, and there an end. And then when the losses begin to mount, there are all different kinds of ways in which they try to manage the crisis and other people suffer. Texts like *Summertime*, seemingly unrelated to tough problems, tackle the impossibility of even stating the problems that would undo solutions for ever.

The first step, then, is to show that the academics, allowed to summarize, are clearly wrong. Sophie, being female, is allowed to speak about the relationship—but she is wrong too. How do we know she is wrong? Let us look at a textual labyrinth again: in a fragment without notes to the reader for what to do in the future, there is a description of education. It is marked as a fragment, saying that it was his mother who put him into Montessori school. If the Calvinist schoolteachers 'had succeeded in forming him' (Sophie has just said that he was a Calvinist. John Coetzee does not know that Sophie has said this. J. M. Coetzee has arranged it so that we will see that Sophie has said it), 'he would more than likely have become one of them himself, patrolling rows of silent children with a ruler in his hand, rapping on their desks as he passed to remind them who was boss' (S: 254). That is an undermining of the first set of fragments, which say: '[I]f you want to succeed in the world and have a happy family and a nice home and a BMW you should try not to understand things' (S: 14). The author tries to stage a critique of phallo-centric heteronormativity by making it a contradiction to the framing fragments at the beginning, which contain various kinds of declarations to the reader: 'He' is a bad word in this consideration of being able to marry, having a proper wife, being a proper husband, having a proper dining table, having proper children and all of that. Almost at the end, there is a peculiar flat idea for a story or novel. Suicide is offered as a kind of controlling or representing of one's own death. A peculiar kind of suicide, where you will swim and swim and swim and swim out into the open sea until the body gives in. He even knows that this will not work, and that is how we end. We end with a peculiarly lame idea of a story which might work, which is not here.

There is of course a rich narrative which ends with Margot. She is the only one who not only remains in South Africa but is also the somewhat feudal person remaining today, trying to run, like Thornton in *North and South*, good, social-ized capital investment—agri-business—a farm that does not quite work because it is kind to all the folks. This is feudal and it is put as such: '*Why are we spending our lives in dreary toil if it was never meant that people should live here, if the whole project of humanizing the place was misconceived from the start?*' (S: 140). It is not a wonderful thing by strict political princi-ples, but the named author is trying to offer it as something which might get more assent. There is violence, however, in the next episode: the killing of Mario, and that line ends in this assemblage of contradictions. And all through runs the heavily sexualized thing, where the character is constantly trying to undo entanglements, making a dreadful, stupid pass at Adriana and hugging tight when Julia says: 'If I were free, would you marry me?' He does the usually straight male thing—the more you reject them, the more they like your technique, as the song went.[5] That is what he does to Margot. When Margot hugs him, he is not able to accept it. He falls in love—in the sense of looking at female physicality. Everyone thinks he is homosexual. The question of 'what is he' is also in with the rest. That line ends with Margot speaking of his capacity to love. Together they redo the common polite way of saying, they are having sex—'sleeping together'— in an interesting and important way in the car, but without, literally, having sex. The episode is important in terms of the text.

Gender and territory, not art for art's sake; self-referentiality displaced in the interest of a truth beyond the politically correct. Therefore, when we come to the end of the book itself, it cannot be accepted as a conventional end. That also has to be laid out. In this book, the patriarchal straight man's desire for Oedipus. What is Oedipus? To overcome the anxiety of influence, to be able to reject the father, to avoid sleeping with the mother, *the* patriarchal story—it is always there as subtext. Mother has been kept in. The important 'end' remains in the

5 Pat Boone, 'Technique' by Johnny Mercer on *Four by Pat* (Dot DEP-1057, 1957), single 7" EP.

middle, working with the female shifter—*her* mother. Not *my* father, not *my* mother; *her* mother.

(In Derrida's *Glas* [1974], the homosexual man's [Jean Genet's] mother cannot be caught in the absence of the patronymic. In the body of the text, you have an L-shaped emptiness—a representation of the French shifter *elle*—meaning 'she'.) This is even further: *her* mother is as far as your can go from the Oedipal. 'She won't know me.' 'Can it stand as it is?' And Margot says in effect, 'I'll have to see.' That open end and the desire to represent the writable. Whereas in *Glas*, it is: 'We cannot know the queer man's mother, but we can make a sign.' The patriarchal system says that the father is the sign, giving the last name from generation to generation. For the mother, it is just the cut in menstrual blood that produces a child. That is the trace, written in blood: first withdrawal, then restoration; in the middle, a making. In other words, the flow of blood continues, nameless, from generating to generating: a sexist position.

You can take it, wear it like a crown, without taking note of all the social problems that come in with it, and that is what happens in the structuring of *Summertime*. If *Disgrace* is hard to accept with the heroic lesbian accepting the child of rape and beginning with nothing, it is because we cannot all be tragic heroes. This is a second try: a benign, good woman relating to the countryside as sacred space, still feudal, trying to humanize but understanding that the failure is not due simply to the failings of the 'Coloured' folk. The book itself cannot end with Sophie's summarizing of the Coloured people. It must end with: '*She won't know me.*' 'Can it stand as it is?' And then Margot.

Another ending: Oedipus. Not a fulfilment of Oedipus. He cannot kill his father but it is an undecidable split. 'There is no other choice, Father. I must either leave you'—his father has been operated on for meningeal cancer; the wound must be looked after and he is the only one who can look after it— 'I must either leave you, or cut my life short in incredibly complicated ways.' This is the representation of parricide. This is the banal predicament of the contemporary, over and against which one cannot just take the old and say, 'That was better,' because the Golden Age is nonsense. This is merely a representation of the Oedipal situation, because of the desire to represent the writable. The Oedipal is history and the trace of the mother in blood is species. Reproductive heteronormative discourse, our oldest institution, is also being approached, and not psychoanalytically. The shrink in the text is put in her place in the very first section. Even this can be placed within the general technique of the withholding of the intertextuality as deep allusion, preparing 'notes towards an unauthorized biography'.

So, an unspecified England, Paris, Sheffield and then an unspecified area called Tokai. 'Watch.' There is some Afrikaans in the Margot section. The Koup, which is, he says, a Khoi word, belonging not to Afrikaans or Zulu or any of the big African languages but to the Coloured. We are told that they are beginning to leave the Western cape. His mother is from the Northern Cape, the book tells us. What is it the Cape of? Good Hope. Why? Rounding it made the passage to India possible. Why the passage to India? Europe fell. Constantinople was taken by the Ottomans. Suez was closed; we must find another way: circumnavigation, the Cape of Good Hope, colonialism, Columbus going the other way, Ottoman envy—continues to this day, as alternative routes to us (in this book, I am an Indian speaking to Indians!) are being sought. Let us not forget *Summertime* as a fable of territory. That fable, as contained in *Summertime*, is universaliz*able* but not universal—in other words, today globalizable but not a candidate for the Hall of Fame of 'world literature'.

Coetzee, whoever he is, wants to be saved by the text. He left South Africa (most people think, although they might be wrong) because the African National Congress, incapable of reading *Disgrace*, implied that he was a racist. He left for Australia, where he says John Coetzee died. This is not just game-playing, and certainly not the Coetzee of 1984 writing on Rousseau.[6] The idea of the fable of territoriality, in terms of the movement of people, is not just isomorphic colonial movement as we would understand it if we kept Indian-American postcolonialism as our model. The Boers are different from the English, and the Khoisan are different yet again. All contained within the fable of reproductive heteronormativity. Which contains this other fable.

Both of these fables are accessed in important ways by both text and narrative. Reported speech as used a la

6 J. M. Coetzee, *Truth in Autobiography* (Cape Town: University of Cape Town, 1984).

Volosinov.[7] We might also mention Freud's remark in *The Interpretation of Dreams* (1899) about dreaming easy dreams so that they could be interpreted to fulfil the desire for interpretation.[8] That is how this author is using this 'postmodern', metanarrative theory here. The use of that theory signals to itself and helps us approach an entire complex: the place of truth, the rewriting of *Disgrace*, the coming away from Cordelia/Lucy as tragic hero, towards the woman with her own faults, the burden of feudalism marked by history and the fable of reproductive heteronormativity; accounting for a man who seems unable to raise a family.[9]

7 V. N. Volosinov, 'Exposition of the Problem of Reported Speech' in *Marxism and the Philosophy of Language* (Ladislav Matejka and I. R. Titunik trans) (Cambridge, MA: Harvard University Press, 1986 [1973]), pp. 115–23.

8 Sigmund Freud, 'The Psychology of the Dream-Processes' in *The Standard Edition of the Complete Psychological Works of Sigmund Freud* (James Strachey ed.), VOL. 4, *The Interpretation of Dreams (First Part)* (James Strachey with Anna Freud, Alix Strachey and Alan Tyson trans) (London: Hogarth, 1958), pp. 509–610.

9 In order to flesh this out with a reading that refers to both South Africa and Coetzee's life story, see David Attwell, 'Trauma Refracted: J. M. Coetzee's *Summertime*' in Michela Borzaga and Ewald Mengel (eds), *Trauma, Memory and Narrative in the Contemporary South African Novel* (Amsterdam: Rodopi, 2012), pp. 283–94.

There are a few cautions that I should advance with reference to this otherwise excellent article. In my reading, an adjective such as 'maudlin' to describe 'life in Tokai' (p. 287) would not be appropriate, and some of Attwell's remarks are too close to Sophie and Martin's summaries. Also, I do not read *Summertime* as a memoir, and what Attwell sees as 'ordinary facts' are, for me, textualized. Attwell's invocation of a 'writerly persona' goes against my conviction of the universal desire for the impossible representation of the writable—more appropriate to Barthes' *scriptible*. I would

QUESTIONS

1. Critical Intimacy

Let me here recapture some of the things mentioned earlier in the book. How does one distinguish between establishing critical intimacy with literary texts and with canonical expository texts? My disciplinary formation is literary criticism. I read everything that way. My own reading will be described, I hope, by other people. I therefore cannot avoid attempting to enter the protocols of the text. The only thing that I do remind my students and myself of is the different relationship to the claim to veridicality in literary texts as opposed to expository texts. In my Columbia seminar on the General Strike, we read *North and South*, Rosa Luxemburg, Du Bois, Gandhi and Tagore, Benjamin, Sorel, Derrida and then, again, a novel, *Tell Me a Riddle* (1961) by Tillie Olsen. I repeatedly told my students that the claim to veridicality was different in the texts. (This relates to the representation of non-contradiction as universal, so that people can recognize the place of truth in Margot in *Summertime*.) I added: 'Always keep in mind that the invitation of the text relates to veridicality in different ways, and we cannot clearly distinguish

also like to think that Coetzee attempts to imagine the narrativity of female narrators as epistemological performance for himself, and I believe that this can be extended to many of his other novels. Finally, I cannot see the effacement of Coetzee's biographical mother as a kind of balancing of accounts. I have offered you, rather, the engagement with the reproductive heteronormativity—her mother—replaying the Oedipal with Oedipus withdrawn. I hasten to add that I engage at such length with Attwell's piece because I respect the kind of authority that his sustained work on Coetzee must carry.

between the literary text as just unverifiable. There is a species of truth-claim or validity-claim, even there.'

Rosa Luxemburg's *Mass Strike* (1906) tries to teach the German Social Democratic Party (SPD) the lesson of Russia, the strongest left party in Europe—Marx's own party—how to read what happened in Russia between 1892 and 1905. This was a desire to give a veridical reading, to help the SPD dislodge itself from a position of power through knowledge. When we were reading the paper on Rosa Luxemburg that was presented by a student, we saw that all he could do was comment on the images. The student did not enter the protocols of the text, which was to teach the union movement, the Party, the well-off proletarians, the subproletarians, each group mentioned in the various chapters, how to read what was happening in Russia and how to interact in the immediate and distant future. On the other hand, people who read only for that kind of summary ignore, for example, that at the end of the text, Luxemburg proposes a kind of eternal return, so that from time to time, the flashpoint of the General Strike will arise, in order that the unions and the Party and the relatively well-off upwardly mobile section of the proletariat who can *think* the Party will see again that in that mobility, madness and bad politics lie.

Looking towards the future, fighting the undecidable, is also a desire for representing the writable, in this case, the immense stream of history. The idea of entering the protocols attentively, looking at the private grammar set up by the text—for example, Luxemburg's use of repetition rather than argument to question Marx and Engels. The sheer force of repetition worked better rhetorically, against the tremendous mockery of *Anti-Dühring* (1878), where Engels dismisses the General Strike, Bakunin and the rest. Marx and Engels' argument is that the General Strike is unnecessary because, if the working class is ready to do a General Strike, it does not need a General Strike. Luxemburg will not dispute with the big authors for social justice and revolution. She is pushing with another technique of teaching, which is to repeat and repeat. She repeats these incredible lists: what factories, what places, what years, over and over again, new lists, new demands, new victories.

When you enter, for example, the protocols of Kant's philosophical texts, you learn that when he says *Grundsatz*, he means founding conditions within the programming of the philosophizing subject. When he says *Princip*, he means the principle in pure reason that understanding cannot touch. He uses Latin in this way, and it is comparable to Marx's use of Latin. Kant, Hegel and Marx—and I am sure other philosophers within the German classical tradition—use *das Verhältnis* in the sense of a correct structural place, and *die Beziehung* as simply any relationship. These are protocols that are not necessarily reasonable rules that apply across all kinds of texts; on the other hand, if we do not know them, it will be difficult for us to read the text's message.

When you achieve something like this critical intimacy, you are in a position neither to excuse (Kant as a racist, Hegel as a capitalist, Fanon as a sexist) nor to accuse (Marx as a racist, Socrates as a sexist, Nehru as a classist) but to locate a place where you think the text will allow you to turn it round and use it—to use its best energies for the project at hand.

No excuses, no accusation. Earn the entry. The generic differences—this is philosophy; this, on the other hand, is literature—are in many ways incidental to people trained in literary reading like ourselves. For me at least, it is just reading —not specifically 'literary' reading any more. Of course, it depends on my disciplinary formation: I cannot philosophize, I cannot write like a historian and I have no anthropological curiosity. Others call me interdisciplinary and I always wonder why. All I can say to my students is: locate the precise claim for the veridical, respect it and then go for the excuse / accuse / use dance, but, in the case of literature, do not give in to the desire to say that it hangs out for its own sake. That comes out of a space and time that has not done the best for us. Even Kant, starting up during nascent capitalism, says that in the aesthetic, we can enjoy our capacity to represent without any objective support and that is the only way we can exercise judgement.

So that remains my answer to the requirement to distinguish between philosophy and literature. The real answer is in three words: I don't know.

CLOSING REMARKS

I bring you back to my opening remarks: on borderlessness. Today, empirically, capital can move in a borderless way all round the globe. This borderlessness which, by a performative contradiction, has to keep borders intact, can be taken as the extra-moral condition of the mode of production which runs us, which we can use to propose a comparative literature borderless in English, which attempts to keep linguistic borders intact by devoted attention to its palaeonymy.

Rather than say, 'Global English cuts me down!', take it and begin to move it so that you can enter other Indian languages—not just your mother tongue—keeping those borders intact for you to breach, because, if you just think of borderlessness, you will move round in inadequate English translations.

Another reminder in my closing remarks is: to treat Hegel's *Phenomenology* not simply as a sequential narrative but also as a spatial epistemograph. That kind of graphic intuition is also in Kant: in his epistemograph, Kant uses grace itself, or rather its effect, a space in the picture of the thinking mind. And in *Summertime*, in the idea of prayer: Margot is

made to say, trying to fulfil the textual desire, that the movement of prayer is not a bad thing. Because, for Kant, mere
reason (rational choice?) is 'morally lazy' and just tries to put
a plus in the place of a minus, we must make a little room
for the effect of grace. Not the cause of grace—because practical reason is merely programmed to speak cause—but just
the effect. I find that this exhortation has quietly entered my
picture of reading: not only to understand by reasonable conduct but the prayer also to be haunted. This is more than just
critical intimacy. Once we get to this difficult effort, ill paid
as you will be, and mocked as you will be, and in a hostile
polity as you are, the task of the teacher of literature, in the
broadest sense, is to restore this insane and competitive,
genocidal, nationalistic place into something like a country
among global countries. We are not in the national-liberation
phase where we have to be the 'best'. We know that neither
national liberation nor competition is a 'revolution'. Therefore, the prayer to be haunted by the country as text brings
us to equality rather than victory as a model. Indeed, if we
affirmatively sabotage Kant's idea of the effect of grace into a
broader structural model of non-religious prayer, it will help
us to keep the fragile structures of secularism alive, without
disavowing the transcendental.

A reminder about the double bind, noticing contradictory instructions, and also noticing how the text pushes you
towards a decision, coaxes you to break the double bind. I
hope you will enjoy this in future, even as you realize the seri-
ousness of this training in reading the other(s) carefully

enough to undertake the rearrangement of desires, your own, and theirs. Be literal, do not turn everyone into yourself, and do not turn literature into evidence of social reality or theory.

Learning from mistakes is another important point. 'Can the Subaltern Speak?' was the beginning of such a process of learning, which has today brought me to a very different place: from the burning of the widows in the past, to the changing of children's mind in the present, for the future— please keep that in mind when you want to praise the essay. In its author's intellectual life, it has served the purpose of opening a door, rather than remaining a monument.

Avoid the fault of the benevolent feudals—anthropologizing the aboriginal by preservation, and thus joining hands with UNESCO and the Nara Document of 1994, to 'authenticate' cultural heritage. Literature authenticates nothing—it runs along, away from evidentiary authentication. A hard lesson—to be learnt over and over again.

Be aware that a desire represented in a text is not its fulfilment. Be aware of the general desire to capture the writerly, the undecidable.

The last thing I will say is, do not tell me, 'This is India!' because it can be done here. If you want to learn languages, you can learn languages. Stay with it. And thank you for making me welcome.

BIBLIOGRAPHY

ANDERSON, Benedict. *Imagined Communities: Reflections on the Origin and Spread of Nationalism*. London: Verso, 2006[1982].

ATTWELL, David. 'Trauma Refracted: J. M. Coetzee's *Summertime*' in Michela Borzaga and Ewald Mengel (eds), *Trauma, Memory and Narrative in the Contemporary South African Novel*. Amsterdam: Rodopi, 2012, pp. 283–94.

B. E. 'Istanbul', *Enclyclopædia Brittanica*, VOL. 22, 15th EDN. Chicago: Encyclopædia Britannica Inc., 1995, p. 148.

BARTHES, Roland. 'Introduction to the Structural Analysis of Narratives' in *Image Music Text* (Stephen Heath trans.). London: Fontana Press, 1977, pp. 79–124.

——. *S/Z*. Paris: Éditions du Seuil, 1970. Available in English as: *S/Z* (Richard Miller trans.). London: Jonathan Cape, 1975.

BATESON, Gregory. 'Double Bind, 1969' in *Steps to an Ecology of Mind*. New York: Ballentine Books, 1972, pp. 271–8.

——. 'Toward a Theory of Schizophrenia' in *Steps to an Ecology of Mind*. New York: Ballentine Books, 1972, pp. 201–27.

BENJAMIN, Walter. 'Critique of Violence' (Edmund Jephcott trans.) in *Selected Writings*, VOL. I, *1913—1926* (Marcus Bullock and Michael W. Jennings eds). Cambridge, MA: Harvard University Press, 1996, pp. 236–52.

———. 'Theses on the Philosophy of History' in *Illuminations* (Harry Zohn trans.). London: Pimlico, 1999, pp. 245–55.

BOONE, Pat. 'Technique' by Johnny Mercer on *Four by Pat*. Dot DEP-1057, 1957, single 7" EP.

BRONTË, Charlotte. *Jane Eyre*. London: Smith, Elder, 1847.

CÉSAIRE, Aimé. *Une saison au Congo*. Paris: Éditions du Seuil, 1966. Available in English as *A Season in the Congo* (Gayatri Chakravorty Spivak trans., Souleyman Bachir Diagne introd.). London: Seagull Books, 2010.

CHATTERJEE, Partha. *Nationalist Thought and the Colonial World: A Derivative Discourse?* London: Zed Books for the United Nations, 1986.

CHIBBER, Vivek. *Postcolonial Theory and the Specter of Capital*. New York: Verso, 2013.

COETZEE, J. M. *Age of Iron*. New York: Penguin, 1990.

———. *Boyhood: Scenes from Provincial Life*. New York: Penguin, 1997.

———. *The Childhood of Jesus*. New York: Penguin, 2013.

———. *Disgrace*. New York: Penguin, 1999.

———. *Dusklands*. New York: Penguin, 1982[1974].

———. *Foe*. New York: Penguin, 1986.

———. *The Life and Times of Michael K*. New York: Penguin, 1983.

———. *Slow Man*. New York: Penguin, 2005.

——. *Summertime: Scenes from a Provincial Life*. New York: Penguin, 2009.

——. *Truth in Autobiography*. Cape Town: University of Cape Town, 1984.

——. *Waiting for the Barbarians*. New York: Penguin, 1980.

——. *Youth*. New York: Penguin, 2002.

CONDÉ, Maryse. *Heremakhonon: A Novel* (Richard Philcox trans.). Boulder, CO: Lynne Rienner, 1982.

CORTAS, Wadad Makdisi. *A World I Loved: The Story of an Arab Woman*. New York: Nation Books, 2009.

DAVUTOĞLU, Ahmet. Interview by Scott Macleod, *Cairo Review of Global Affairs*, 12 March 2012. available at: http://-www.aucegypt.edu/gapp/cairoreview/pages/articleDetails.aspx?aid=143 (last accessed on 18 april 2014).

DELEUZE, Gilles, and Félix Guattari. *Anti-Oedipus: Capitalism and Schizophrenia* (Robert Hurley, Mark Seem and Helen R. Lane trans). Minneapolis: University of Minnesota Press, 1983.

DERRIDA, Jacques. 'Force of Law : The "Mystical Foundation of Authority"' (Mary Quaintance trans.) in David Gray Carlson, Drucilla Cornell and Michel Rosenfeld (eds), *Deconstruction and the Possibility of Justice*. New York: Routledge, 1992, pp. 3–67.

——. *Glas* (John P. Leavy and Richard Rand trans). Lincoln: University of Nebraska Press, 1990[1974].

——. *Of Grammatology* (Gayatri Chakravorty Spivak trans.). Baltimore, MD: Johns Hopkins University Press, 1974.

——. *Of Spirit: Heidegger and the Question* (Gregory Bennington and Rachel Bowlby trans). Chicago: University of Chicago Press, 1989.

——. 'The Violence of the Letter: From Lévi-Strauss to Rousseau' in *Of Grammatology* (Gayatri Chakravorty Spivak trans.). Baltimore, MD: Johns Hopkins University Press, 1976, pp. 101–40.

DEVI, Mahasweta. 'Breast Giver' in *Breast Stories* (Gayatri Chakravorty Spivak trans.). Calcutta: Seagull Books, 1997, pp. 39–76.

——. 'The Hunt' in *Imaginary Maps* (Gayatri Chakravorty Spivak trans.). New York: Routledge, 1995, pp. 1–18.

——. 'Pterodactyl, Puran Sahay, and Pirtha' in *Imaginary Maps* (Gayatri Chakravorty Spivak trans.). New York: Routledge, 1995, pp. 95–196.

DICKENS, Charles. *Hard Times*. Cambridge: Riverside, 1869.

DJEBAR, Assia. *Fantasia: An Algerian Cavalcade* (Dorothy S. Blair trans.). London: Heinemann Educational Books, 1993.

——. *Far from Madina: Daughters of Ishmael* (Dorothy Grant trans.). London: Quartet, 1994.

DU BOIS, W. E. B. *Black Reconstruction in America: Toward a History of the Part Which Black Folk Played in the Attempt to Reconstruct Democracy in America, 1860–1880*. San Diego, CA: Harcourt, Brace, 1935.

——. 'The Negro Mind Reaches Out' in Alain Locke (ed.), *The New Negro: Voices of the Harlem Renaissance*. New York: Atheneum, 1992, pp. 385–414.

ENGELS, Friedrich. *Herr Eugen Dühring's Revolution in Science*: *Anti-Dühring* (Emile Burns trans.). New York: International Publishers, 1935.

FANON, Frantz. *Black Skin, White Masks* (Charles Lam Markmann trans.). London: Pluto Press, 2008[1986].

———. *The Wretched of the Earth* (Richard Philcox trans.). New York: Grove Press, 2004[1963].

FOUCAULT, Michel. 'Le Dispositif de Sexualité' in *Histoire de la Sexualité, I: La Volonté de Savoir* (Paris: Éditions Gallimard, 1976), pp. 107–73. Available in English as 'The Deployment of Sexuality' in *The History of Sexuality*, VOL. 1, *The Will to Knowledge* (Robert Hurley trans.) (London: Penguin, 1978), pp. 77–131.

———. Preface to Gilles Deleuze and Félix Guattari, *Anti-Oedipus: Capitalism and Schizophrenia* (Robert Hurley, Mark Seem and Helen R. Lane trans). Minneapolis: University of Minnesota Press, 1983, pp. xi–xiv.

FREUD, Sigmund. 'Beyond the Pleasure Principle' (1920) in *The Standard Edition of the Complete Psychological Works of Sigmund Freud* (James Strachey ed.), VOL. 18, '*Beyond the Pleasure Principle*', '*Group Psychology*', *and Other Works* (James Strachey with Anna Freud, Alix Strachey and Alan Tyson trans). London: Hogarth, 1955, pp. 7–64.

———. 'The Psychology of the Dream-Processes' in *The Standard Edition of the Complete Psychological Works of Sigmund Freud* (James Strachey ed.), VOL. 4, *The Interpretation of Dreams* (*First Part*) (James Strachey with Anna Freud, Alix Strachey and Alan Tyson trans). London: Hogarth, 1958, pp. 509–610.

——. 'The Uncanny' (1919) in *The Standard Edition of the Complete Psychological Works of Sigmund Freud* (James Strachey ed.), VOL. 17, *From the History of an Infantile Neurosis* (James Strachey with Anna Freud, Alix Strachey and Alan Tyson trans). London: Hogarth, 1955, pp. 217–56.

GANDHI, Mohandas K. 'The Poet's Anxiety' in Sabyasachi Bhattacharya (ed.), *The Mahatma and the Poet: Letters and Debates between Gandhi and Tagore, 1915–1941*. New Delhi: National Book Trust, 1997, p. 66.

GASKELL, Elizabeth. *North and South* (Alan Shelston ed.). New York: W. W. Norton, 2005.

GRAMSCI, Antonio. 'On Education' in *Selections from the Prison Notebooks* (Quintin Hoare and Geoffrey Nowell Smith eds and trans). London: Lawrence and Wishart, 1971, pp. 26–43.

HABERMAS, Jürgen. 'Conservative Politics, Work, Socialism and Utopia Today'. Interview by Hans-Ulrich Beck, 2 April 1983 (Peter Dews trans.) in Peter Dews (ed.), *Autonomy and Solidarity: Interviews with Jürgen Habermas*. London: Verso, 1991, pp. 131–46.

——. 'Modernity Versus Postmodernity' (Seyla Ben-Habib trans.). *New German Critique* 22 (Winter 1981): 3–14.

HEGEL, G. W. F. *The Phenomenology of Spirit* (A. V. Miller trans.). Oxford: Oxford University Press, 1977.

HEIDEGGER, Martin. 'The Origin of the Work of Art' in *Poetry, Language, Thought* (Albert Hofstadter trans.). New York: HarperCollins, 1971, pp. 15–86.

——. *What Is Called Thinking* (Fred D. Wieck and J. Glenn Gray trans). New York: Harper and Row, 1968.

JOYCE, James. 'The Dead' in *Dubliners*. New York: Viking, 1967[1914], pp. 175–224.

———. *Finnegans Wake*. London: Faber and Faber, 1939.

KAFKA, Franz. *Letters to Friends, Family and Editors* (Beverly Colman, Nahum N. Glatzer, Christopher J. Kuppig and Wolfgang Sauerland eds; Richard and Clara Winston trans). London: Oneworld Classics, 2011[1977].

———. *The Trial* (David Willey trans.). New York: Dover Thrift Editions, 2003.

KAKAR, Sudhir. *The Inner World: A Psychoanalytic Study of Childhood and Society*. New Delhi: Oxford University Press India, 1978.

KANT, Immanuel. 'What Is Enlightenment?' in *Kant On History* (Lewis White Beck ed. and trans.). New York: Macmillan, 1963, pp. 3–10.

LACAN, Jacques. 'The Subversion of the Subject and the Dialectic of Desire in the Freudian Unconscious' in *Écrits: A Selection* (Alan Sheridan trans.). London: Routledge, 2001, pp. 323–60.

LEVI, Primo. *The Drowned and the Saved* (Raymond Rosenthal trans.). London: Michael Joseph, 1988.

———. *Survival in Auschwitz, and The Reawakening* (Stuart Woolf trans.). New York: Summit Books, 1986.

LEVINAS, Emmanuel. *Otherwise than Being, or Beyond Essence* (Alphonso Lingis trans.). Pittsburgh, PA: Duquesne University Press, 1998.

LUKÁCS, Georg. *The Theory of the Novel* (Anna Bostock trans.). Monmouth: Merlin, 1971.

LUXEMBOURG, Rosa. *The Mass Strike* (Patrick Lavin trans.). Detroit, MI: Marxian Educational Society, 1925.

MACKENZIE, Jean K. (ed.), *Friends of Africa*. Cambridge, MA: United Study of Foreign Missions, 1928.

MAJUMDAR, Kamalkumar. *Antarjali Jatra* (The Final Journey). Calcutta: Subarnarekha, 1981.

MANTO, Saadat Hasan. 'Toba Tek Singh' (Khalid Hasan trans.) in *Memories of Madness: Stories of 1947*. Delhi: Penguin, 2002, pp. 517–23.

MARAIS, Eugène. *My Friends the Baboons*. London: Blond and Briggs, 1975[1939].

MARX, Karl. *Capital: A Critique of Political Economy* (Ben Fowkes trans., Ernest Mandel introd.), 2 VOLS. New York: Vintage, 1977.

——. *Economic and Philosophical Manuscripts of 1844* (Martin Milligan trans.). New York: Prometheus Books, 1988.

——. *The Eighteenth Brumaire of Louis Bonaparte* (Clement Dutt trans.) in Karl and Marx and Friedrich Engels, *Collected Works*, VOL. 11. New York: International Publishers, 1990, pp. 99–197.

——. 'Theses on Feuerbach (III)' in *Karl Marx and Frederick Engels: Selected Works*, VOL. 2 (Moscow: Foreign Languages Publishing House, 1962), pp. 403–4.

MELVILLE, Herman. *Moby-Dick*. New York: Bantam Classic, 1981[1851].

NAIPAUL, V. S. *India: A Million Mutinies Now*. London: Heinemann, 1990.

——. *The Mimic Men*. London: Penguin, 1987[1967].

Nietzsche, Friedrich. *On the Genealogy of Morals* (Walter Kaufmann and R. J. Hollingdale trans). New York: Random House, 1969.

Olsen, Tillie. *Tell Me a Riddle* (Deborah Silverton Rosenfeld ed. and introd.). New Brunswick, NJ: Rutgers University Press, 1995[1961].

Ovid. *Metamorphoses* (David Raeburn trans.). London: Penguin, 2004.

Proust, Marcel. *In Search of Lost Time* (C. K. Scott Moncrieff, Terence Kilmartin and Andreas Mayor trans, D. J. Enright revd.), 7 VOLS. New York: Random House, 1992[1922–31].

Rhys, Jean. *Wide Sargasso Sea*. New York: W. W. Norton, 1966.

Rilke, Rainer Maria. 'I, 9' in *The Sonnets to Orpheus* (Leslie Norris and Alan Keele trans). Columbia, SC: Camden House, 1989, p. 9.

Said, Edward. *Orientalism*. London: Penguin, 2003[1978].

Sanil V. 'Spivak: Philosophy'. Lecture delivered at the Department of English, University of Pune, 11 December 2007.

Schiller, Friedrich. *On the Aesthetic Education of Man* (Reginald Snell trans.). New York: Dover Publications, 2004.

Sen, Aparna. *36 Chowringhee Lane*. DVD. Directed by Aparna Sen. Bombay: Eagle Distributors, 1981.

Shakespeare, William. *King Lear* (R. A. Foakes ed.), The Arden Shakespeare Third Series. Walton-on-Thames: Nelson, 1997.

Soga, John Henderson. *The Ama-Xosa: Life and Customs*. Alice: Lovedale Press, 1932.

SPIVAK, Gayatri Chakravorty. 'Can the Subaltern Speak?' in Cary Nelson and Lawrence Grossberg (eds and introd), *Marxism and the Interpretation of Culture*. Urbana: University of Illinois Press, pp. 271–314.

———. 'To Construct a Personal Past: Pages from a Memoir'. Dilip Kumar Roy Memorial Lecture, Sri Aurobindo Institute of Culture, Calcutta, 9 July 2010.

———. 'Getting a Grip on Gender'. Lecture delivered at Atelier Genre Condorcet, Paris, 10 July 2013.

———. 'Lie Down in the Karoo: An Antidote to the Anthropocene', review of *The Childhood of Jesus* by J. M. Coetzee, *Public Books*, 1 June 2014. Available at: http://www.publicbooks.-org/fiction/lie-down-in-the-karoo-an-antidote-to-the-anthropocene- (last accessed on 8 August 2014).

———. *Nationalism and the Imagination*. London: Seagull Books, 2010.

———. 'Nationalism and the Imagination' in *An Aesthetic Education in the Era of Globalization*. Cambridge, MA: Harvard University Press, 2012, pp. 275–300.

———. 'Penny for the Old Guy'. *Cambridge Review of International Affairs* 27(1) (2014): 184–98.

———. 'Planetarity' in *Death of a Discipline*. New York: Columbia University Press, 2003, pp. 71–102.

———. 'Preface to the Routledge Classics Edition' in *Outside in the Teaching Machine*. New York: Routledge, 2009, pp. xiii–xiv.

———. 'Reading *De la grammatologie*', preface to *Reading Derrida's 'Of Grammatology'* (Sean Gaston and Ian Maclachlan eds). London: Bloomsbury Academic, 2011, pp. *xxix–xxxix*.

———. 'Rethinking Comparativism'. *New Literary History* 40(3) (Summer 2009): 609–26.

———. 'Righting Wrongs'. *South Atlantic Quarterly* 103(2–3) (Spring–Summer 2004): 523–81.

———. 'Terror: A Speech after 9/11' in *An Aesthetic Education in the Era of Globalization*. Cambridge, MA: Harvard University Press, 2012, pp. 372–98.

———. 'Thinking about Edward Said: Pages from a Memoir'. *Critical Inquiry* 31(2) (Winter 2005): 519–25.

———. 'Three Women's Texts and a Critique of Imperialism'. *Critical Inquiry* 12(1) (Autumn 1985): 243–61.

———. 'Translation as Culture'. *Parallax* 6(1) (2000): 13–24.

STERNE, Laurence. *The Life and Opinions of Tristram Shandy, Gentleman*. New York: Dover Publications, 2007[1759].

STOW, George. *Native Races of South Africa: A History of the Intrusion of the Hottentots and Bantu into the Hunting Grounds of the Bushmen, the Aborigines of the Country* (George McCall Theal ed.). London: Swan Sonnenschein, 1905.

TAGORE, Rabindranath. *The Home and the World* (Sreejata Guha trans., Swagata Ganguli introd.). New Delhi: Penguin, 2005.

THIONG'O, Ngugi wa. *Globalectics: Theory and the Politics of Knowing* (*Wellek Library Lectures*). New York: Columbia University Press, 2012.

VISWANATHAN, Gauri. *Masks of Conquest: Literary Study and British Rule in India*. New York: Columbia University Press, 1989.

VOLOSINOV, V. N. 'Exposition of the Problem of Reported Speech' in *Marxism and the Philosophy of Language* (Ladislav Matejka and I. R. Titunik trans). Cambridge, MA: Harvard University Press, 1986[1973], pp. 115–23.

WILLIAMS, Raymond. 'The Industrial Novels' in *Culture and Society, 1780–1950*. London: Penguin, 1961[1958], pp. 87–109.

YEATS, W. B. *Collected Poems of W. B. Yeats*. London: Collector's Library, 2010.

———. 'The Great Year of the Ancients' in *A Vision*. London: Macmillan, 1962[1937], pp. 243–66.

———, and T. Sturge Moore. *Their Correspondence, 1901–1937* (Ursula Bridge ed.). London: Routledge & Kegan Paul, 1953.

ZIAHDEH, Khaled. *Neighbourhood and Boulevard: Reading through the Modern Arab City* (Samah Selim trans.). New York: Palgrave Macmillan, 2011.